$6 95

D0121977

A Sierra Club Totebook®

Wilderness Skiing

by Lito Tejada-Flores
and Allen Steck

Drawings by Alfred Smith

Sierra Club   San Francisco • New York

Copyright © 1972 by the Sierra Club.
All rights reserved.
Library of Congress catalog card number 72-89120.
International Standard Book number 87156-069-0.
Produced in New York by Harold Black Inc., and printed in the United States of America by Fred Weidner & Son Printers, Inc.

Contents

Introduction

Why *Wilderness Skiing*?

The 'why' of this book is simple. Skiing off the beaten track has been our passion for years. And, through ski instructing and leading trips to remote mountain areas of the world, we've discovered that introducing other people to our mountain passions is almost as exciting as enjoying them ourselves. And sometimes more rewarding. We hope this book will be such an introduction for many potential friends that we'll never meet in person.

The 'why' of the title is a little more involved. There are standard expressions to describe this sport: *ski touring* and *cross-country skiing*. But they are often limited to one particular technique of skiing. We had thought of *mountain skiing* as a general catch-all until we started counting all the days we had spent on Nordic skis, without gaining or descending more than a hundred vertical feet. Still, we wanted something to distinguish our subject from just plain skiing. *Wilderness Skiing*, at least, has the right feeling.

The 'why' of our sport (and it is not just a sport) is even more subtle. There are a thousand positive whys and more than just a few will become evident in this totebook. But there is at least one very important negative reason why our subject doesn't simply come under the heading: skiing.

Like everything else, skiing has changed, and like everything else, this change has not necessarily been for the better. The proliferation of lodges, of on-the-slope restaurants, snack bars and warming huts; the ever-present mechanical spiderwebbing of lifts, crossing and crisscrossing the slopes; the ever-longer lift lines, more evocative of a subway at rush hour than of a traditional mountain scene;

the trail markers and hazard warnings and skier-traffic signs that echo the urban street corner—this is what surrounds us today on America's ski slopes, from Vermont clear through the Rockies to the Sierra. And what is the nature of the sport we practice so diligently, so enthusiastically, in this white arena? Some exciting moments, to be sure, flashing, turning or tumbling down well-groomed slopes. But the rest of our time, the other two-thirds or, on a crowded weekend, three-quarters of our skiing day, is spent waiting in line or riding back up the hill in the mechanical embrace of a steel chair or a claustrophobic metal cabin. How easy to understand the cynical epithet used by a few to describe the winter sport of the many: 'yo-yo skiing'.

But wait a minute. This book is not simply another complaint about how things are no longer what they used to be. Wilderness skiing is alive and well in America, but it no longer means just getting a pair of skis and learning how to use them. Wilderness skiing, as opposed to just plain skiing, is defined by environmental contrast and experienced only by conscious choice.

Wilderness skiing, as we understand it, practice and love it, and hope to explain it in this book, is any form of skiing away from the confines of an organized ski area—any sort of skiing that takes place, and takes the skier, far from the madding crowd. It is not one homogeneous sport, but rather a whole variety of feelings, of excursions, of movements: walking, plodding under giant packs; loping and gliding through forests; sliding endlessly down gentle glaciers and spring snowfields; plunging through steep forests, down long chutes. It may last for hours, days or weeks at a time.

There are only a few common threads. Snow, of course,

in its infinite variety of depths, types, expanses and terrains. A pair of skis on one's feet—but here again what a variety of choices. A reliance on one's own muscles for movement, and on one's judgment and one's friends for security. Finally, and perhaps above all, a sense of escape, of astonishing freedom, of heading *out*, of breaking out of restrictive patterns (whether an urban life-style or just a set of recreational habits) into a white universe where surprise is constant, into an environment that erases and re-draws itself continuously from early winter long into spring. Wilderness skiing is a passport that lets one travel freely from the seasonless city into a 'beyond', generally so difficult of access and seemingly so hostile, that it has been spared the invasions which have nearly urbanized the American outdoors in summer.

Though not outrageously difficult, wilderness skiing is one of the more demanding, more esoteric, least obvious ways of behaving in a wild environment. Almost certainly this is why it offers so much and why it is practiced by so few in proportion to, say, knapsacking. With this handbook we hope to make wilderness skiing less esoteric, though no less demanding. And if the growing snowmobile danger can somehow be headed off, the back country in winter should remain, for a long time to come, America's wildest wilderness.

This is the mystique of wilderness skiing. The solitary cross-country skier, who devotes a couple of morning hours to run a few miles through Adirondack forests, shares it. The family or small group on an all-day tour to some frozen lake, some nearby summit, shares it. The powder freak, who hikes away from the ski area for a few miles to get a perfect untracked run, shares it. The ant-like figures of an expedition, toiling up a long Alaskan glacier on their short skis, share it. The mountaineer, descending to camp on *firngleiters* after a spring ascent, shares it. Frenchmen on the crevassed slopes and steep passes of the *Haute Route*, and Scandinavians on featherweight skis crossing flat, white plains beneath the Arctic Circle, all are sharing this same mystique—snow-covered landscapes where men seem out of place, with only skis to discover their secrets.

Of course, one must first learn the secrets of the skis themselves; one must first come to terms with these slippery, awkward and at first unmanageable sticks strapped to one's feet. There are other secrets, too, to be learned before one can feel at home in the mountains in the winter. A glance at the Table of Contents will show just how much there is that one *can* learn. But first things first. For us, the first thing is motion, getting there and getting back across the snow, and enjoying it; in other words—skiing.

If you are already an accomplished skier, expert or merely competent, Nordic or Alpine style, so much the better. You can skip the first few chapters. Our first task in this handbook, however, is to introduce the neophyte or non-skier to the basic techniques of skiing as simply and safely as possible. There are several initial choices open to the beginner or would-be wilderness skier, and these are explained in chapter 1, *The Two Styles*. Expert skiing of any style is quite difficult, but fortunately it doesn't take long to acquire a minimum level of proficiency for touring, and learning to ski is generally more fun than it is frustrating.

There are other ways of getting around in a snowy mountain landscape than on skis. Snowshoeing in particular comes to mind, and is not without its own staunch advocates who claim a long list of practical advantages for these ancient, honorable but somewhat ungainly contraptions. Hopefully the snowshoer too will find helpful winter techniques in this book, but our subject was and remains wilderness skiing. A narrow bias, perhaps, that we justify on two grounds. First is our conviction that skiing, even in unpacked and variable snow conditions, is not hard to learn. Second, and even more important, is the extra dimension of kinesthetic involvement with the landscape that only skiing provides: the quality of the sport in its rhythmic, controlled yet free movement. And also the purely esthetic quality of ballet-like passage through a fantasy environment—all the more beautiful for having no spectators other than the unblinking stillness of the mountains themselves.

Imagine a predawn start, a long climb through frozen air, up into sunlight, high above timberline, a sharp sunlit summit, a feathery cornice and then—the long run down: endless linked esses, turns, traverses, long straight runs down velvety silent snowcapes. Live this once, and wilderness skiing will become your thing as it has become ours. We hope this book will shorten the struggles of your apprenticeship and speed you on your trip.

How to use this book

Wilderness Skiing is a common-sense sort of handbook. In writing it, we have tried to avoid the usual overly compartmentalized, overly rational division of topics. Instead, you will find Nordic ski equipment, together with Nordic ski technique for beginners and advanced skiers, all in the same chapter. In the same way, stoves, cooking gear, nutritional theory and practical winter cooking, all fall together as a logical section of our chapter on multi-day ski tours. We hope this arrangement will make things 'come together' a little easier, and save you a lot of skipping back and forth through the book.

Wilderness Skiing is divided into three parts. Part I, THE TECHNIQUES OF WILDERNESS SKIING, is the most important. It is the 'how-to-do-it' portion of the book. How to ski, how to ski in difficult and tricky conditions, how to camp out in winter, how to melt water and cook in the snow, how to organize your ski tours, how to travel efficiently and safely through the mountains in winter.

Parts II and III are more for general reference than for actual instruction. Part II, THE WILDERNESS SKIER'S ENVIRONMENT AND ITS HAZARDS, covers the basics of mountain topography, orientation and weather, and the story of snow, its physical characteristics and its chief danger—avalanches. In particular, how to recognize and avoid, or deal with avalanche danger. And, in the last chapter of this section, a summary of emergency medical and evacuation procedures, stressing typical ski and winter injuries.

Part III, THE INFINITE VARIETY OF WILDERNESS SKIING, is designed to expand your horizons beyond the local touring scene. It is a general guide to the type, feeling and location of ski-touring areas in different regions of the United States and Canada. Also, in this section we try to sketch-in some basic information on what to do when slopes steepen, and mountain skiing merges gradually into mountaineering.

The appendices contain much useful information in the

form of lists, all of it too dull for easy reading but too important to leave out.

We suggest a careful reading of part I, omitting either chapter 2 or 3 (depending on your choice of Nordic or Alpine skiing styles), and only a general perusal of part II, except for chapter 7 on avalanches, which should be thoroughly mastered. Part III is more esoteric than important. Use it as needed, or read it merely to whet your appetite for distant snowfields.

Part I.
Techniques for Wilderness Skiing

1. The Two Styles

So let's put on our skis and get started.

Not so fast. Not only must we first select our gear and learn how it works, but there is one very important question to answer. *What style of skiing will we be doing*? This needs some explanation. Briefly there are two main styles of skiing: Nordic skiing and Alpine skiing. As far as the back country goes, Nordic skiing is often called 'cross-country' skiing, and Alpine-style skiing is described as ski touring. But these are just words. What is the real difference between the two styles?

The fundamental difference between Nordic and Alpine skiing is in the equipment used. Nordic equipment is extremely light and flexible, while Alpine equipment (both boots and skis) is heavier and more rigid. Both, of course, have their advantages, and this is because a distinctly different style of movement has developed in the use of the two kinds of gear. Each style has its own problems, satisfactions and rewards, and each is fundamentally suited to different types of terrain. There are other differences such as cost of equipment and ease of learning. But first, a quick look at each side.

Nordic or 'cross-country' skiing, as the name implies, is the style of skiing popular in the Scandinavian countries— Finland, Norway and Sweden—where very open, predominantly flat or gently rolling terrain has influenced the development of the sport. The idea, the very point of Nordic skiing has always been travel—getting from here to there—and not necessarily climbing up something, or somewhere, in order to enjoy an exhilarating run back down.

The technique for just plain traveling that has evolved in

Scandinavia is astonishingly dynamic, graceful, and almost easy. An experienced cross-country ski runner can eat up the miles as though they weren't there. His technique is a direct result of his equipment: longish, extremely slender, lightweight wooden skis, waxed in such a way that they glide forward yet grip the snow for climbing and 'kicking' (more on this mysterious phenomenon in chapter 2). These light, whippy skis are attached to the toe of an equally light, slipper-like boot or shoe (often cut below the ankle) by the simplest of binding systems. This permits a total flexing of the foot so important to the free striding movements of the cross-country skier.

Alpine skis, on the other hand, are a good deal wider than Nordic skis, and are equipped with sharp steel edges. Perhaps due to the greater commercial possibilities of the sport, Alpine skis have undergone much greater technological development and innovation, and today are made of hybrid metal-fiberglass-foam combinations more often than of wood. Alpine boots are stiffer and higher, and the bindings offer a means of attaching the foot rigidly to the ski (although Alpine 'touring' bindings do allow heel lift for the uphill and level parts of the tour). Why such differences?

Once again, the name tells all. This equipment, and the style of skiing associated with it, developed in the Alps, on steep, rugged, often precipitous terrain. Merely to get down some of the steeper slopes in the Alps was, initially, a great challenge; and as technique developed and equipment evolved, Alpine skiing drew further away from its Scandinavian origins (the earliest known skis are from Lapland). Skiing downhill became not just another aspect of the sport, but its main point. This is the reason for the heavier, stiffer equipment. Because of it, the Alpine skier enjoys much greater control (and often security) on steep, rugged, icy or otherwise difficult terrain. But he has sacrificed lightness and freedom of movement on easy ground.

This is not the whole story. Nor is the difference between the two styles absolute and final, especially when considered as simple techniques, as means for experiencing what we've called wilderness skiing. More and more often, we see experienced cross-country skiers, or ski mountaineers, blending and combining the techniques of the two styles to fit their own ambitions, skills and terrain. Nordic waxes, for example, can be used on the plastic bases of Alpine skis. And there are bindings available which permit the use of heavy mountaineering boots with lightweight Nordic skis. This eclecticism, however, is not for the beginner. The first steps in learning either Nordic or Alpine skiing are pretty well cut-and-dried, and represent separate and distinct (though not contradictory) approaches. So if we're going to learn to ski, we'll have to choose. On what grounds?

The first are geography and terrain. Logically, the East and Midwest, with their more gentle mountainscapes, lend themselves to Nordic touring. Vertical relief is a must for Alpine skiing, so if you plan to ski primarily in rolling fields and forests the choice is obvious. In the Rockies and the West, a great case can be made for using Alpine equipment and techniques. Not only is the terrain often very steep, but higher altitudes tend to produce trickier snow conditions, giving the edge to the Alpine style, at least on the descent. There is however, enough gentle-to-intermediate terrain in these western ranges so that Nordic touring is beginning to experience a real surge of interest. So terrain, we see, is important but not decisive.

More important is your ambition and your general out-door experience. What is your personal vision of ski touring or wilderness skiing? Are you a newcomer to the mountains? Or do you already feel comfortable bushwhacking over steep passes during long summer backpacking trips? Are you perhaps an experienced climber, hoping to extend your climbing season year-round? If your ambitions are modest, if you're not already fascinated by steep terrain, not already a downhill skier or a would-be winter alpinist, then *begin with Nordic ski touring.*

Nordic skiing is in no way a second choice. It's an extremely practical way of moving over the snow. It has its own esthetics and its own charm, but most of all, it has a special advantage for the beginner—it is very, very easy to learn.

Naturally, a good instructor, or a friend who is both skilled skier and patient explainer, can speed things immensely. Still, under the worst learning circumstances, we feel that an average healthy person can become competent with Nordic cross-country skis in a few days. With Alpine gear, especially in untracked snow, minimum mastery might take weeks, or longer. This is not to say that after a few days on Nordic skis you will be doing the same things that an Alpine skier learns to do in the course of a season. The whole challenge of Alpine skiing is learning to turn down the hill on a variety of terrain. Nordic skis aren't really designed to turn very well anyway (though it is possible) and once you've got the hang of the basic level stride, there's nothing to stop you from taking off on your first all-day tour.

One other factor argues strongly in favor of beginning your career as a wilderness skier with Nordic equipment—its remarkably low cost. Of course, outfitting oneself with Alpine touring equipment is much cheaper than becoming a well-dressed, well-equipped downhill skier (with $200 skis and $150 plastic boots) but Nordic cross-country gear is still the cheapest there is. Before you buy anything, however, we advise trying to rent or borrow all you need for the first weekend, just long enough to see if it's really your thing.

Whichever way you decide to start, with Nordic style skiing (read chapter 2) or with Alpine style skiing (read chapter 3), as you go on to become an accomplished and enthusiastic wilderness skier, don't neglect the other alternative. Each offers special possibilities, special pleasures, and special thrills, that the other style cannot. Perhaps the most complete wilderness skier is the one who adapts himself most perfectly to the kind of landscape he is moving through. Becoming too ardent a champion of one style or the other can only limit your winter's experience. But now we've got a lot of learning to do. Let's begin.

2. Nordic-Cross-Country Ski Techniques

Entire specialized volumes have been written on the mysteries of Nordic skiing, although usually with an emphasis on racing and not touring. In this chapter, we don't try to compete with such works. Rather, under the headings of *Equipment, First Steps* and *Advanced Techniques*, we hope to give a concise summary of Nordic skiing—selecting your gear, waxing, a simple approach to learning the basics, and some obvious refinements, all geared especially to the needs of touring away from a prepared track (the Nordic equivalent of a packed slope). Unfortunately, you can't become an expert by studying a text like this. But you can make a lot of progress, even on your own.

Equipment

In the last few years there has been a minor explosion in the availability of Nordic ski gear in this country. In the 'good old days' one bought whatever was available. But now it's necessary to know exactly what you want, in order to choose from an astonishing variety of categories and models of equipment. Nordic gear is quite specialized; one cannot simply make do with old ski equipment lying around the attic and call it Nordic just because it looks funky. Fortunately, for the most part, good Nordic gear is quite cheap.

SKIS: Correct ski length is to the break of the upraised wrist (the pole, from floor to armpit). Nordic skis are classed in three categories: racing, light touring, and touring

skis. Racing skis are quite narrow, very light and fragile—
unsuitable except for skiing on a prepared track. Light
touring skis retain much of the racing ski's narrowness and
springiness, but are heavier due to a much stronger construction. The touring ski, per se, is a catch-all, varying
from a slightly wider ski, to one almost as wide as traditional downhill models. Some, the so-called 'mountain skis,'
even have metal edges usually only associated with Alpine
skis. This is only a rough breakdown, for innovation in the
design and construction of Nordic skis has tended to blur
some of the classical distinctions. Naturally, we recommend
only the light touring and touring models to the would-be
wilderness skier.

Traditional Nordic skis are wooden, generally laminated
and often have hard bottom edges of 'lignostone' (compressed beech wood). Despite their narrowness (48 to 52
mm wide for light touring skis) they have both *camber*
(bottom curvature) and *side camber* (a narrow cut at the
'waist' or center) just like downhill skis. The bottoms or
'soles' of these skis are of birch or hickory, ideal for holding
the special waxes which make Nordic skiing possible. These
wooden skis range in price from $25 to $50 and still
dominate the market. Light touring skis made of wood
weigh 3 to 4 lbs; heavier touring skis 5½ to 6 lbs. a pair.
Almost all these skis are imported and some of the better-
known brands are Jarvinen, Bonna, Sundin, Madsus, Rex,
Edbyns, Oy, Sandstrom, Bla-Skia and Splitkein. The import
picture is in a state of flux, however, and in a few years we
may be buying the same skis under different names.

The situation is also changing with the rapid development of new materials. Wooden bottoms demand a good
deal of care and preparation, and several manufacturers

have recently produced a new type of treated plastic base which, they claim, holds wax as well as the classical pine-tarred ski. And fiberglass, which offers unquestionable advantages of lightness and strength, has lately been used to build the whole ski. Fischer, Toko, Kneissel and the American company, Hexel, are all marketing skis in this category. While not yet fully accepted for Nordic racing, many of these fiberglass or fiberglass-reinforced skis, with light-weight, hollow or foam cores, make excellent touring skis—especially for long trips to remote areas where a broken ski would be more than an inconvenience. The corresponding disadvantage is obvious: they cost up to twice as much.

Another new category is even more ingenious, and more controversial: the no-wax ski. There are two kinds. One, marketed by Trak and Attenhoffer, has a plastic 'fish-scale' base—an overlapping pattern of disks, stamped into the plastic, like an upside-down shingle roof. Another kind has two thin strips of mohair set permanently into the plastic base on either side of the traditional center groove. Both these bases permit you to climb without sliding backwards, but they seem to sacrifice one of the hallmarks of a well-waxed ski, the good glide on the flat. The fish-scale base is quite fast on straight downhill run; but the fish scales wear rapidly on hard snow, and should you ever have to wax them (and you probably will), removing old wax from the scales becomes a real chore.

These skis may, however, be just right for certain purposes. For example, if you're very impatient, and view skiing only as a way of getting somewhere rather than an end in itself; or for certain mountaineering trips; or if you habitually tour with a very large pack which would curtail your gliding stride—then the 'no-wax' ski is great. Inciden-

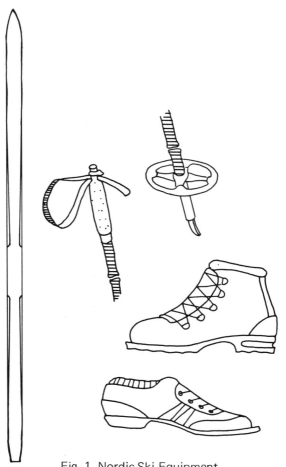

Fig. 1. Nordic Ski Equipment

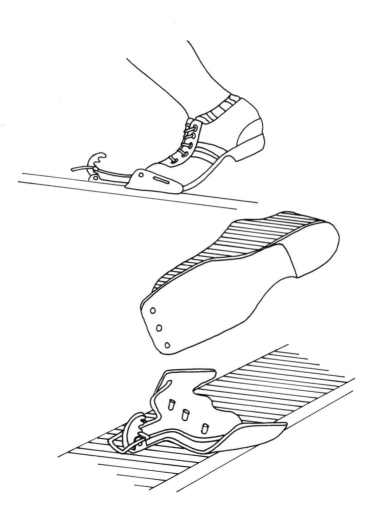

tally, waxing is not really one of the negative aspects of the sport. It has its own mystique and, believe it or not, its own pleasures which we'll get to soon.

Which type of ski to choose? For most people we would recommend a modest, wooden, light touring ski ($20 to $40). They aren't much harder to balance on than the wider touring ski. And if you're going to get into Nordic skiing, go all the way and experience the unique feeling that one only gets with these slender boards. Fiberglass and plastic skis (at $50 *and up*) are skis that an experienced skier chooses for a special purpose. If possible, try to rent skis your first few times out, and in this case the no-wax models might be an advantage (when they're available) in giving you one less thing to think about at first.

BOOTS: Nordic boots follow the same three types: racing, light touring and touring. They are all flexible single-thickness boots whose soles (sometimes leather but more often a composition material) usually have three small holes, drilled or grommeted near the toe, to accommodate the pin-type toe-clamp binding which is becoming standard. The racing boot (or shoe) resembles a track shoe, cut very low beneath the ankle. The light touring boot is cut above the ankle. And the touring boot is slightly higher, slightly heavier, and generally has a notched heel to accommodate cable bindings as well as the toe-clamp type.

If you live in the West, where deep snow is quite common, or if you plan to do some long multi-day tours, we strongly advise the so-called touring rather than the light touring model. It will keep your feet a good deal warmer, and generally gives a little more lateral support for edge control when crossing rugged terrain and skiing downhill. The lower-cut light touring boot is adequate for one-day tours and gentle terrain, and is ideal for skiing in a track.

Additionally, you can use a heavy climbing boot with the wider Nordic skis, by means of the Silvretta binding. But this is a case of using Nordic skis to go somewhere, rather than actually doing Nordic cross-country skiing which requires extremely flexible shoes. This is one of a number of good mountaineering solutions which we'll cover later. Nordic ski boots are not expensive despite their quality leather and workmanship and retail for under $35. Some well-known brands are Lake Placid, Alfa, Jette, Askim, Kikut, Riber and Trak.

BINDINGS: These are the cheapest part of your touring outfit, costing from $5 to $10 (whereas leading release bindings for downhill skiing are now over $60). There are two main types. The toe-iron type which holds the boot at the toe only, leaving the heel completely free. And the 'Tempo' type cable binding, even simpler than the cables formerly used in downhill skiing—the cable passes around the heel and connects to the toe irons, but doesn't hold the heel down on the ski. The Silvretta cable binding just mentioned is an exception, offering hooks to hold the heel down during the descent, but partially inhibiting its free movement on the level—a compromise, not a specific Nordic solution. If you borrow or rent skis, of course, you can use those with cable bindings, like the Tempo. But for learning and general Nordic touring, we definitely recommend the classic pin-type toe-iron binding. Go Nordic all the way.

This classic binding works by means of three small pins that match three holes in the toe of the boot sole, together with a simple wire or metal fork that holds down the boot's large square welt, and locks into a metal catch just ahead of the toe. The number of pins formerly varied and one had to drill the boot holes oneself, but size and spacing have now been standardized and most boots fit most bindings.

A heel plate should be put on the ski as well. These are small metal squares or vees, often with a rubber 'pop-up' in the center. They keep snow from balling up underfoot. But even more important for the touring skier, the serrated metal edges help to keep your heel from slipping sideways when turning downhill.

There are even step-in Nordic toe bindings available nowadays. But they require permanent mating of one pair of boots to one binding, as the boot toe is equipped with a special metal plate. Several of our friends have tried them and then gone back to the classic pin-type binding. Besides, one of the charms of cross-country skiing is its relative freedom from gadgetry.

POLES: Nordic poles are longer, lighter and whippier than downhill poles. They have a curved metal point at the bottom and a simple rounded handgrip, and should have adjustable wrist straps. Nowadays the light plastic basket (or ring) is replacing older cane and leather ones. The cheapest poles are of bamboo and are perfectly adequate (under $10). The fanciest ones are the Scott duraluminum poles at about double that price.

WAX AND WAXING: Waxing, in its theory and in practice, is the big mystery at the heart of Nordic skiing. People who have done some downhill skiing are invariably amazed at the idea that one wax can make your skis stick while going up, and also make them slide faster going downhill, and even more fantastic, do both of these things in the course of a single stride. This is how it works.

Snow, even hard icy spring snow, does not have a smooth

surface, but a microscopically rough one, composed of snow crystals in their original state or in various stages of breakdown and transformation. The waxed surface of a ski, likewise, presents a certain roughness and irregularity; further, the wax may be more-or-less soft or porous, permitting the snow crystals actually to penetrate as well as to interact and catch on the rough surface. Typical downhill waxes present a very hard surface which the snow cannot penetrate, and thus they only accelerate the skis. Some waxes in the cross-country range, on the other hand, are so very soft, and snow crystals interact with them to such a degree, that if used on the wrong snow, you can't slide at all.

The correct wax for a given condition represents a compromise: soft enough to grip when the ski is at rest and weighted, yet just hard enough so that, once in motion, the crystal structure of the snow can't snag and hold the passing ski. (An engineer or physicist will realize that these Nordic waxes take advantage of the fact that static friction is always greater than dynamic friction.)

In specifying which wax to choose, the manufacturer's instructions and waxing charts always list the type of snow, and the temperature (which alters the humidity of the snow). The three main types of snow (as far as waxing is concerned) are: *new snow* whose crystals are in their original state; *settled snow* which has smaller more compacted crystals from settling under its own weight; and *old snow* (also called *granular* or *metamorphosed snow*, and often 'spring' or 'corn' snow) i.e. snow that has been transformed by repeated thawing and freezing into a form of granular ice with small, rounded, lumpy crystals. Obviously, new snow with its sharp crystals will grip wax better, and so

requires the hardest wax. Similarly, old snow will normally
need thicker, softer wax. In addition, each category can
range from cold and dry to warm and wet. And since any
water in the snow forms a lubricating layer between the ski
bottom and the snow surface, we naturally use a softer wax
the wetter or warmer the snow. But unlike waxing for a
downhill race, it's usually sufficient to look at the air
temperature, not the snow temperature.

So much for theory. How does all this work in real life?
Preparing and waxing the skis involves several steps. If the
skis have wooden bases, they must first be cleaned of any
protective factory coating and then sealed with some kind
of pine-tar compound. This protects and waterproofs the
ski and also helps the wax to adhere. Spray-on and paint-on
preparations are available, but purists (and experts) seem to
prefer heating the pine tar into the ski with a torch. It's a
tremendously messy job, but one that somehow makes you
feel like an old pro even before you've put your skis on for
the first time. This will be your first introduction to the
faithful butane cartridge torch which is a valuable part of
the cross-country waxing kit. A lot of grief can be saved by
wiping on only a thin coating of tar to start with. Then,
after applying the tar, heat it till it just bubbles and quickly
wipe off the excess with a rag. If you keep the flame of the
torch moving, you won't burn the wood of your skis. The
sealed, pine-tarred skis should feel slightly tacky when
touched.

Next comes the base wax or binder. This is an intermediate coat of soft, slow wax which will help the final wax to
adhere longer. This base is important in racing, but is
generally ignored by touring skiers, although it can be a
help if you ski on consistently rough snow. It can be heated

on in a thin layer and should be reapplied several times a season.

Now, the heart of the subject: the running wax. This is what you actually ski on, and this is where the decision-making and expertise of waxing resides. There are virtually a dozen different brands of wax available in this country, with each manufacturer making a complete range for all conditions. Rex, Rode and Swix have been popular brands, and recently Toko, the Swiss company which has a large corner of the downhill wax market, has been making a major effort to get its cross-country waxes into American shops. Aside from availability, one advantage of these four brands is that their color-coding is nearly identical, i.e. a blue or violet stick wax in one line is about the same as in another. Even so, the beginner would be well advised to pick one brand of readily available wax and master its secrets before experimenting.

These waxes come in two forms: *hard* or *stick waxes* in little cans, and sticky liquid waxes or *klister* in tubes. *In general, use hard wax for new and settled snow, and klister for old or granular snow* (snow that's undergone repeated thawing and freezing). Hard waxes are generally rubbed on and smoothed out with a cork. Klisters are squeezed on in a thin layer and smoothed out with a metal scraper, but the torch can be used in both cases for a smoother job. Manufacturers' waxing charts and instructions are certainly adequate, so we won't go into more detail here, except to list a few points that beginners should remember.

Wax indoors, with skis at room temperature, and then allow the skis to cool outside before skiing. Skis must be scraped clean of old wax before applying new wax. When in doubt between two waxes, choose the harder of the two; if you can't get enough 'kick' or grip, you can always apply soft wax on top of hard, but not vice versa. If you're going skiing for a few hours only, a thin layer of wax should suffice. If you're planning a long day's tour, you'll need more wax, but multiple thin layers are more effective than one thick layer. And finally, don't get discouraged if the wax doesn't seem to work correctly during the first few steps; one often has to ski for several minutes, or several hundred yards, before the wax is properly 'run in'.

Before leaving this subject, we should mention some non-traditional waxes, and underline a few of the limits of waxing for touring. Several all-purpose waxes are available: sometimes just one wax to be applied in differing thicknesses; a two-wax package like Bratlie's Gold and Silver; or even Aerosol-can spray-on waxes. These seem fine for beginners who are not yet demanding enough nor knowledgeable about a good wax job. The best of these simpler waxes that we have used is Toko ski touring wax in a white-topped can. It has a bubble-gum like consistency, and applied thickly underfoot will get you up almost anything.

This brings up the last point: even the best wax will not work everywhere. Indeed, most cross-country waxes are designed more for running in a packed track, over consistent snow, than for skiing in untracked and variable snow conditions. Variable is the key word. For if conditions are too variable you may find yourself sliding backward for a few steps and then being almost unable to move forward. Breakable crust is one such condition, with a slick icy surface on top, and fluffy light powder underneath when you break through. This past winter, friends returning from long ski tours (one in Alaska, one across the Sierra) told us some pretty frustrating tales about days when no single wax

or combination of waxes would work, even though they
had miles to cover. When conditions change, rewaxing on
the trail, in the cold, can be a drag, if not a major problem.
Removing klister, especially, can be a real task on the trail.
And for this reason, back-up hard waxes like the Toko
touring wax just mentioned can be invaluable. Some people
have gone so far as to modify a pair of mini climbing skins to
use with Nordic gear on long-range mountain jaunts. If
you're carrying a large pack, losing your glide isn't much of
a sacrifice, as heavy loads tend to reduce skiing to mere
plodding; and one can wax 'soft' for climbing, then rub a
little paraffin on the skis for the downhill stretches.

The beginner, reading about cross-country waxes, is usually boggled. Don't worry, it's not *that* complicated. In
fact it's more like an intriguing puzzle where no two skiers
come up with the same solution.

First steps

Nordic skiing is one of the few sports where a self-taught
participant can hope to achieve reasonable proficiency.
Technically, it's quite simple, and the advanced skier distin-
guishes himself by his stamina, rhythm and the perfection
of a few basic movements, rather than by performing a
separate class of advanced maneuvers.

Nordic or cross-country racing is done on a course or
track, which is no more than a set of solidly packed ski
tracks. This track guides the skis directionally and frees the
skier to concentrate on perfecting his stride. In Scandinavia,
a great number of these tracks are laid out and maintained,
and when someone goes off for a day's cross-country skiing,
he may well spend it on such a track. Skiing in a track is

not as confining as it sounds, but there are very few such tracks in this country outside of centers where there is an interest in cross-country racing, for which the track is a *sine qua non.* It's probably safe to say that more people in this country use Nordic gear for just grooving around in the woods than skiing on a track.

It's often said, as well, that touring technique doesn't differ from good racing technique, and that the only way to learn cross-country skiing correctly is on a track. We disagree. Running on a track with experienced Nordic skiers is a valuable experience. Breaking a trail may be more fatiguing, but its *your* trail, and quite satisfying. The following is a sequence of steps we suggest for mastering your Nordic skis (even though it isn't the only way).

THE BASIC STRIDE: Start your learning on the flat. A meadow is great, and the snow conditions should not be too deep, crusty or otherwise tricky, though a little powder is fine. Put on your gear and start walking around. At first, just shuffle your feet forward on the snow. Use your poles for balance and to prop yourself up if you start to tip over. To turn, just shuffle slowly around in a wide circle—because a quick movement, stepping your foot to the side, will result in crossed skis. Now, as you get used to the skis, try walking in a straight line, as evenly and smoothly as possible. Let your arms swing, just as in hiking or walking down the street, and plant your poles alternately, with each step. If you're relaxed, you will find that as you step forward with your right foot, your left hand also swings forward. Plant your left pole in the snow and give yourself a little push as your left foot and right hand come forward.

This natural movement of opposite hand and foot is the

Fig. 2. The Basic Diagonal Stride

basis of Nordic skiing's most important technique, the so-called diagonal stride. To get the feeling of the diagonal stride, you have to change your slow shuffling forward movement into a more dynamic stride, into a *kick* and a *glide*. Try to do this bit by bit, as soon as you feel comfortable in a brisk walk. Still heading in a straight line, push off from one foot onto the other and, balanced on this new ski, let yourself slide to a stop. Then repeat, pushing off this ski back onto the other which you thrust forward, and once again try to ride this new front ski as it slides over the snow. (See fig. 2)

Kick, the Nordic expression commonly used to describe this driving off one ski onto the other, is a little misleading to the beginner, although it's clear enough when you see an expert striding along. Instead of kicking anything, or throwing your back foot out in the air like a bucking mule, simply try to push forward off the ground with a vigorous extension of your leg. Equally important in the 'kick' action, and needed to produce the long glide on the front ski, is the forward drive of your hand and the *knee* of the other leg (the one you're pushing onto, the one on which you will glide). But don't try to feel all this at once. Just lengthen your strides, make them more dynamic, feel your weight moving forward from one ski solidly onto the other, and don't try to rely too much on your poles for forward push. As in hiking, climbing, or even downhill skiing, the legs must do most of the work.

As soon as your stride loses its wobbly quality and you leave a fairly straight set of tracks (skis comfortably apart, neither wide nor narrow stance), turn around and practice the diagonal stride in your own tracks. If the snow surface is easy to move around on, you may want to go off on a mini tour after a few minutes' practice—it's that easy! But we would advise a couple of hours skiing on the flat before looking at any hills, where you'll encounter a new set of problems.

HELPFUL MANEUVERS: Before you tackle some easy hills, there's a tricky maneuver you can try on the flat—the *kick turn*, which will be very handy later. It's used to turn around, 180 degrees, in place. The secret is to support yourself solidly on your poles, yet lift them, one at a time, out of the snow, to let your skis past. Instead of describing the kick turn (like describing a pretzel) we'll just refer you to figure 3. To start, it helps to swing your foot back, before kicking it straight up; but if this maneuver gives you trouble, don't be upset. The kick turn is very awkward, and not too important at this stage, even though it is a basic tactic for cautious ski tourers. A very steep and justly famous peak at Squaw Valley, California, is known as KT-22, because the first party to ski it used 22 kick turns to link their descending traverses.

Fig. 3. The Kick Turn

Also before we tackle hilly terrain, you might practice falling and getting up a few times. If you haven't fallen over yet, you soon will. Falling on Nordic skis is extremely safe, compared to the high leverage Alpine gear exerts on your legs. But you should still work on falling comfortably and safely to the side: land on your seat, and use both poles to help yourself up. Since the heel is not held down in Nordic bindings, it's easy to fall forward, and this is the worst direction to fall, though you probably don't risk more than a sore toe (from your foot being held into the bindings at the toe). Running downhill, try to fall back and into the hill.

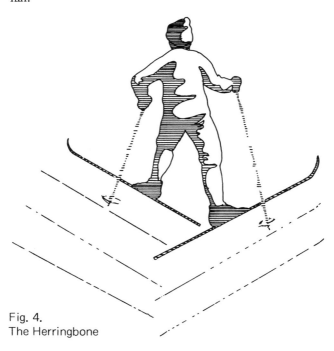

Fig. 4.
The Herringbone

Fig. 5.
The Sidestep

Enough of falling. Up we go. You will be amazed that you can walk straight up gentle to moderately steep slopes without sliding back. At a certain steepness, depending on the snow and your wax, you will begin to have difficulty gripping. Solve this problem by slapping your skis down onto the snow instead of shuffling them up on the surface, and keeping your knees and ankles well bent so that your weight rests on the whole ski rather than just on the tails. If your diagonal stride is coming along fairly well, try *skiing* up the slope instead of just walking up, by shortening your strides into a kind of bouncy, aggressive dog trot. But this is usually too much for first-time beginners. In any case, when you reach the point where your skis no longer grip (or before, for comfort's sake), here are some other ways to keep climbing.

You can spread your ski tips in a wide vee. Then, dishing the skis inward on their edges, keep walking straight up, using your poles behind you as props (see fig. 4). From the tracks it leaves, this method of climbing is called the *Herringbone*. It is very fatiguing, though less so with Nordic skis than Alpine ones, and only useful for short distances.

Easier and slower is the *sidestep*. This one is obvious. Place your skis horizontally across the slope and walk them up one at a time, as though climbing a staircase sideways like a crab—make the uphill edges of your skis grip the slope by rolling your knees and ankles inward if necessary. If the snow is soft, don't worry about edging. Just stomp on up and, by using your poles alternately for balance, you will soon catch the rhythm. (See fig. 5). Although it doesn't take much effort, side-stepping is so slow that one has the sensation of never getting anywhere, and for this reason, the next method is the most popular.

Traversing means moving on a diagonal across the slope, either diagonally up, or diagonally down. This is a popular and useful way of avoiding the rigors and occasional frights of the vertical or (as skiers call it) the *fall line*. Traversing doesn't need much explanation. You tack back and forth up the slope in a series of zig zags, choosing an angle of ascent that seems comfortable or practical. The zigs are linked to the zags by a simple stepped turn, on the uphill side, if the slope is not too steep; or, on steeper slopes, by a proper kick turn facing downhill (by kicking the downhill leg around first). Much the same method is often used for going downhill, but there are other problems. Let's see.

DOWNHILL RUNNING: For a beginner, the first thing in skiing downhill is not to scare yourself. Skis accelerate rapidly and that out-of-control feeling is always lurking in the subconscious of the inexperienced Nordic skier. So pick a small hill or a gentle wide-banked gully for your first slides, with a good run-out where you can glide to a stop. Unless you're in a prepared track, we recommend the following position: wide stance, skis about as wide as your hips; ankles, knees and hips loosely flexed, so you are slightly crouched; weight distributed evenly over the flat of your feet, or slightly more toward the heel (as one can topple forward easily); and finally, hands widespread for lateral balance. It sounds complicated but you'd probably assume this position by yourself anyway. It feels secure, and it is. Now push off, glide down the hill and let your skis come to a stop on their own. Then back up and repeat your little straight run, or *schuss*, several times. Try to stay loose and relaxed, feeling where your balance really is, and enjoy the sensation of free movement down the hill. When *schussing* with Nordic skis, it's traditional to advance one ski ahead of the other. But we don't think it necessary or even useful, except in the case of riding over gullies and dips, where parallel ski tips might have a tendency to bury themselves in the snow.

   Now, how about control on a downhill run? Frankly, as a beginner, your control will be marginal and even Nordic experts don't look as graceful and controlled when skiing

Fig. 6. The Step Turn:
from a straight run to a
gentler traverse, but
also used for stopping.

downhill as do their Alpine brethren. The skis aren't designed for easy turning, nor is that the real essence of the
sport. But with a little strategy, your downhill runs will be
both safe and exhilarating.

First, let's master the *step turn*. Try it first as you reach
the flat from a gentle hill. With all your weight on one ski
(the left ski if you are turning right), lift the other ski off
the snow and step the tip out at a divergent angle. Then
transfer your weight to that divergent ski, (i.e. step on it).
And, finally, lifting the first ski, bring it parallel to the one
you're standing on. Then repeat the whole business till

you're pointing the way you desire. Or till you stop, if you're turning uphill to stop. Remember not to step the whole ski wide to one side, but merely change its angle by moving the ski's tip to the side. (See fig. 6). After a few times, you will be able to do this effectively enough to avoid small obstacles. What's more important is to be able to stop by stepping up at the end of a slanting downward traverse. Then you compose yourself, do a kick turn, and start off in a descending traverse the other way. For traversing downhill we recommend the same wide stance, and it's also a help to push your uphill ski as much as a bootlength ahead of the other. After you can descend moderate hills

under control, a whole range of easy tours is within your reach.

One more thing. As soon as possible, but not necessarily the first few times out, learn the *snowplow* for slowing down and stopping, and the *snowplow turn.* This maneuver, in which the skis are held in a wedge to increase friction, is described in detail in the chapter on Alpine skiing. It works just the same on Nordic skis, except that the softer boots make it somewhat harder to edge the skis. So the Nordic skier must use a wider snowplow, and must shift his weight to push on the outside ski in a turn, while the Alpine skier merely steers with his stiff boots. In light snow or on a hard surface, the snowplow is easy and effective. In deep or difficult snow, you will be using a simple basic combination for some time: *traverse, step turn to stop, kick turn, and then traverse again.* Even good skiers often do. But now that we're no longer beginners, let's see what else good skiers do.

Advanced techniques

What is the feeling of advanced Nordic skiing? It's hard to capture something like this in a few words. But it seems to us that in Nordic skiing, the expert level represents perfection in the way you *work* with your muscles to cover terrain; while in Alpine skiing, perfection is found in the way you *control* the outside forces of gravity and friction as you slide down a slope. We have already said that a cross-country master uses the same stride and techniques as the novice, but the difference is incredible. The expert simply functions at a higher level of efficiency.

How to become an expert Nordic skier? It takes a lot of

time, a lot of days, seasons and heaven knows how many kilometers of skiing. Many touring-oriented wilderness skiers will become very competent without ever becoming experts in the technical sense. As with Alpine skiing, we suspect that real technical mastery of the sport only comes from racing, or learning from others who have gone through the athletic discipline of racing. Of course, this is a book on skiing the back country, not becoming an 'expert' skier, and fortunately touring doesn't demand precision skiing in any sense. Freedom of movement, safety, self expression, fun—these are our goals. But if Nordic skiing becomes your passion and you want to improve your technique, there is no substitute for working out with top skiers on a well-prepared cross-country track. You will learn secrets of movement and a sense of *tempo* or dynamic pace that will escape you in untracked snow with a pack on your back. Even so, there are a few definite techniques and pointers for more advanced Nordic skiers that we can discuss:

PERFECTING YOUR STRIDE: The diagonal stride is the basic way a Nordic skier covers ground. It is not really as simple as we made out in our advice to beginners. Take another look at the sequence illustration in figure 2. Is this the way you're skiing? Do you get a full extension with your driving leg? Does your poling hand relax its grip as it passes your body, so that the pole doesn't bob up like a flagpole? Where do you plant your pole? At random, or slanting backward at the same level as your 'kicking' foot to get the strongest push? Do you feel tippy? Or is your body quiet and stable as you move forward? And above all, do you drive your whole weight forward on the gliding ski?

It will take another skier with a critical eye, friend or

teacher, to pick out your mistakes. A very common one is being lop-sided: you will do something different on the right than on the left side, as almost everyone does. Another very common fault is dissipating your energy off to the side, especially by flailing your poles around; arms and poles should work close to the body. Spread them wide for balance on a downhill run, but not while poling. Cross-country skiers in a track generally use a version of the downhill tuck or 'egg' position, arms held compactly in front of them. But the track gives them stability, and this position is quite impractical with a pack. Apropos of packs, you'll discover that they change the feeling of everything. You can still do an effective diagonal stride, but only the strongest skiers really 'kick and glide' with a heavy pack, and then, not all day long.

Double poling is an important variation. It gives great speed on a slight downhill where otherwise you would barely slide, and is useful for varying the rhythm of your pace. It's pretty obvious how to double pole (see fig. 7),

Fig. 7. Double Polling

and it can be used alone to propel the skier who just stands on his skis, or actively in combination with the alternating kick and glide.

Cross-country racers have also developed some interesting variations on the basic stride for climbing hills, but somehow, on an actual tour, we've never run up any hills. It's too much work. Don't forget that for all this talk about dynamic gliding strides, it's no disgrace to just walk on your skis as you did the first day. On an actual tour, your speed and stride will be a function of snow conditions and terrain, how much you're carrying, and perhaps most important, your physical condition. Exercising judgment in the effort you put out, and avoiding exhaustion, is also part of advanced Nordic skiing.

On a tour, you can also use some subtle judgment in picking the route you will take up a ridge or a slope. Avoid sidestepping up long steep hard surfaces, as it's very tiring to edge the skis with light flexible boots. For the wax to hold, you want the whole bottom of the ski to be on the snow, so when traversing upward on a hard surface you may have to roll your ankles *out* a bit to flatten the skis completely. Look at the slope before attacking it, and determine the line of least resistance that leads to its summit.

ADVANCED TURNS: The Nordic skier's bag of tricks for skiing downhill is not limited to the step turn and snowplow turn we've already mentioned. Although not really designed for it, these slender skis will make all the same kinds of turns that Alpine skis do, if one knows how. In general, conditions must be pretty good. On frozen corn snow that's been thawing in the sun for a couple of hours to that particular velvety texture, you feel as if you could do anything.

After the snowplow turn comes the *stem christie* or as it's now being called, the *basic christie* and then the *wide-track parallel turn.* Skiers who have started Nordic skiing with a good background in Alpine skiing pick these turns up right away. Many Nordic ski tourers, who haven't done any downhill skiing, never get them, and it doesn't slow them down a bit. In fact it's more in the nature of Nordic skiing to traverse across slopes, taking a little more time to let the scene soak in, than to try to carve your initials on the slope in the form of a perfect set of tracks down the fall line.

If you want to try these *christies*, or skidded turns, look at the descriptions in chapter 3. They are done exactly the same on Nordic skis with a couple of variations. You cannot steer as strongly with your boots, so you must make more use of unweighting, stepping and hopping your skis to the side. Once a turn is started, you must transfer more weight to the outside ski, and at the same time weight your heels more to push the skis around. You can't do this at all without an anti-skid type heel plate, to keep your heel from twisting off the ski. In short, you will be using an old-fashioned downhill technique which dates back to the days when Alpine boots were almost as soft as your Nordic boots. This technique is characterized by hopping, weight shift, and heel thrust; and the only reason Alpine skiers no longer stress these elements is that their equipment has changed. Angulating the knees and ankles into the hill to make the edges grip is also a part of this technique, and you'll have to do this too on hard snow. In any case, always utilize the wide stance. If you have cable bindings with side hitches to hold your heels on the ski, then you'll really be using Alpine techniques on the descent. For more detail, read the next chapter.

An advanced turn which is purely Nordic is the *telemark*. It carries us even further into the past than the technique described above, and it's a matter of open debate among Nordic specialists whether or not it's still really useful for anything. It's very graceful in powder, and it might really help you someday in a weird snow condition you can't handle any other way (deep wet snow). Advance one ski until you are kneeling on the other or trailing one. Then push the front ski at an angle across the other one, and you'll turn. This one sounds simpler than it really is (see fig. 8).

Fig. 8. The Telemark Turn

Finally, unskiable snow. The limits of downhill technique are reached more quickly on Nordic skis than on Alpine ones. Almost any snow is skiable in the sense that you can get through it; although we recommend that, at any cost, you avoid steep icy slopes on light touring skis. There are, however, a number of snows where it's virtually impossible, or impractical, to make turns downhill. The worst of these is breakable crust; a hard thin layer which breaks in a jagged edge on top, dumping you into deep fluff or mush underneath. In this stuff, it may be necessary to make shallow traverses to keep your speed way down, fall over to stop, then kick turn and repeat.

So one can't ski everything on Nordic skis. Does that matter? Think of all you *can* ski: how easy, how graceful it is, how free you feel with this lightweight gear. There are a great variety of ways you can put mere technique to use, in the context of long or short ski tours. If Alpine skiing doesn't interest you for the moment (we hope someday you'll master both) then skip the next chapter and turn directly to Chapter 4, on one-day ski touring.

3. Alpine Touring Ski Techniques

The whole subject of Alpine ski technique, it seems to us, is more complex than that of Nordic technique. An accomplished Alpine-style skier has mastered a repertoire of many more maneuvers than his Nordic counterpart; he may not do each of these things as well, but there are more of them to do. Indeed, in many books on Alpine ski technique, it's hard to grasp the basic thread, or underlying principles that make things work, beneath the welter of separate turns, *christies* and assorted maneuvers.

By restricting ourselves as much as possible to the problems of skiing unpacked snow, we've tried to make the subject a little simpler. The basic principles are not complicated: a natural wide stance, steering movements with legs and feet, while balancing with arms and poles. It sounds easy. But we must warn the beginning Alpine skier that he will take more falls and feel a little more frustration than the Nordic beginner usually does. One perfect run in deep powder, however, should reassure you that it was all worth it.

The multiplicity of different turns and techniques gives Alpine skiing an intriguing puzzle-like quality; and you will eventually be able to define your own personal technique. Instruction and equipment are more readily available for Alpine skiing, though this may change. But even the choice of equipment is amazingly complex.

Equipment

Alpine equipment tends to be somewhat more expensive

Fig. 9. Alpine Ski Equipment

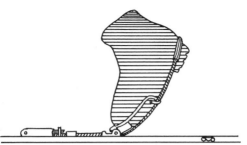

The Silvretta Binding

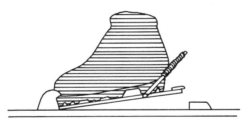

A 'Plate' Type Binding

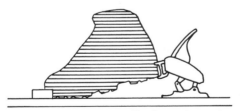

The Su-matic Binding

than Nordic gear, but there are a few corners you can cut in getting set up, and still have first-class equipment.

BOOTS: Alpine touring boots, ideally, are of about the height and stiffness of heavy mountaineering boots. And so, in many cases, if you already own a pair of really heavy climbing boots, these will do just fine. The only problem is whether the heel has a sufficiently large 'ledge' or overhang to accept the cables that are usually used in Alpine touring bindings. Even if they don't, a good shoemaker can often modify them by carving a slight notch for the cable, or one can nail on the sort of metal heel protector designed to go with Nevada Grand Prix bindings, and this should do the trick. A pair of doubled mountaineering boots, made especially for winter climbs, like the Galibier *Hivernal* or the Lowa *Hiebler* models, are ideal. The inner boot of felt provides extra stiffness, and can be quickly dried after a long day in wet spring snow.

Equally high on the list of low-budget preferences are a pair of old-fashioned lace-up ski boots—definitely out of place among the modern six-buckle, plastic, foam-injected models that have become standard on the packed slopes. These boots, also, are generally doubled, but the inner is usually not removable. A lot of skiers still have these old, soft boots lying around in the back of their closets, and often try to get rid of them for ridiculously low prices at annual pre-season ski swaps. Boots like the old Molitor, Haderer, Strolz and Kastinger models are fantastic handmade examples of a lost shoemakers' art. They will last for years and make great touring boots.

Then there are boots specifically made for Alpine ski touring. They are much harder to obtain in this country than in Europe, but major outdoors suppliers have a few models. Some are single thickness boots, some are doubled, and some (like the *Minaret* boot) have vibram soles which can be an advantage for occasional mountaineering. The best special Alpine touring boots, like the Galibier *Haute Route* and the Val d'Or touring boot, are double boots with a removable padded inner, and a unique lace and buckle combination on the outer boot. This permits a very loose comfortable fit for level and uphill sections, and a much tighter fit (plus greater lateral support) with the buckles done up for downhill runs. This is really the ideal, but such boots cost from $50 to $100.

An extremely tight fit in a touring boot can lead to cold feet, blisters and other problems. Yet a loose boot sacrifices control. Obviously a good fit is a compromise, and most touring skiers prefer to use two pairs of socks to retain sufficient warmth *and* snugness.

SKIS: Skis for Alpine touring also offer quite a range of advantages and prices. Although they are generally conventional Alpine skis, of the kind displayed in every ski shop in the country, the touring skier is looking for certain special qualities—light weight (if possible), a very soft flex, only a slight camber, and a somewhat shorter length than normal. His skis will have the usual hidden steel edges and a plastic 'P-Tex' base. Since climbing will be done with 'skins,' the low wax adherence of plastic is not a major factor.

The lightest Alpine skis are the fiberglass models with predominantly hollow cores, such as the Hexel or the Durafiber skis. But although excellent for touring, these skis are outrageously expensive (all over $200). More practical are metal and fiberglass skis of so-called standard construction: a kind of sandwich with a wooden core between metal or glass sheets.

For years, many companies like Head and Hart produced a standard metal ski—actually a beginner's model, which the average skier outgrew in a couple of seasons. These metal skis have largely been replaced by fiberglass ones, but Head Standards are readily available at the ski swaps (held by clubs and ski promoters in October and November), for very low prices: $25 to $45 for used skis in fine condition. The Head Standard is a notoriously soft-flexed ski which makes it ideal for Alpine touring. Soft flex and low camber produce an easier handling ski in deep and heavy snow. An expensive ski of this type is the Miller Soft.

Wooden Alpine skis, which have virtually disappeared from the market, cannot really be recommended, even if you find them. To ski well and to 'hold' on icy slopes they must be quite stiff, and this makes them awkward in deep snow. An exception to this rule is the wide 'mountain ski' made in Scandinavia, with its old-style screw-on edges and usually a wood rather than a plastic base. Fine examples of this type of ski are the Jarvinen Retke Mountain and the Bonna Mountain. These skis are fairly light (6½ lbs.) and easy to handle, and represent an interesting 'middle term' between the classic spectrums of Nordic and Alpine equipment.

A new sort of ski has appeared recently in Europe but is rarely if ever imported to North America. Typified by Rossignol's *Haute Route* model it represents the latest in plastic ski technology applied to the needs of the Alpine touring skier, and available at a moderate price. This type of ski is lighter and softer-flexed than average, with longer, more turned-up tips than usual, for breaking trail in crusty snow.

What about short skis? Experiments with short skis for teaching in recent years have led to some new and interesting models; but most of these GLM skis (for Graduated Length Method) are too flimsy, too short and too unstable for serious touring. A possible exception is the Kneissel GLM ski, which is both wider and thicker than average. It skis well in all snow, but is inherently slower than standard models, though easier to turn. There is also a whole family of super-short mini skis, often called *firngleiters* which are very popular with European mountaineers for descending late-spring and summer snowfields. These are not for serious wilderness skiing, as they are almost worthless for travel in deep snow—but can add a lot of fun to a summer trip if you already know how to ski.

There is, however, a lot to be said for a shorter ski. It's easier to turn and, of course, it weighs a little less. So we recommend buying your touring skis roughly 10 cm. shorter than your normal size in Alpine skis. (Length is determined nowadays more by weight and strength than by the older raised hand method.) So an average strong man who would use a 205 cm. or at most a 210 cm. ski, would take a 195 or 200 cm. touring ski. Wilderness skiing is generally not a high-speed affair. What one loses in stability with slightly shorter skis, is more than compensated for by greater ease in turning. And somewhat shorter skis are still perfectly adequate for deep snow.

BINDINGS: Alpine touring bindings don't allow us any money-saving shortcuts. Their function is more complex than Nordic bindings. For level and uphill touring, they must let the foot flex and the heel rise; yet immobilize the foot and heel for skiing downhill—while also giving an element of security to this now rigid system by a safety release mechanism. There are two main types: cable bindings, and the more sophisticated but not necessarily better step-in models.

Cable bindings still seem more practical, and at the moment the best seems to be the Silvretta binding (see fig. 9). It is unique in that it works just as well with climbing boots as with ski boots (due to the flexible wire toe irons). It also permits unlimited heel lift, as the entire binding (toe irons and all) pivots vertically on a hinge just in front of the toe. The only disadvantage has been a slight loss of lateral or sideways control, when the heel is free on hard slopes. This problem is solved by the Silvretta Plate model, in which a metal plate is added to the cables to give more rigidity, especially with softer boots. The whole unit sells for around $25.

Other cable bindings, the sort popular in downhill circles before the advent of step-in safety release bindings, can also be modified for touring. One must make sure the binding has two sets of side hitches, near the toe as well as the heel, for walking as well as downhill skiing. And one must also fit the ski with some kind of removable toe iron, in addition to the safety toe-release unit (Marker, Nevada, etc.) to keep the foot from wobbling on uphill stretches. If you buy as touring skis a second-hand pair already equipped with cables, then go ahead and modify them. Otherwise we suggest buying and installing the Silvretta, rather than trying to jury-rig a touring binding from scratch. While not a safety binding, per se, the toe guides of the Silvretta will probably bend and deform before the skier is injured from torsion at the foot. There is one safety-release toe-iron of the old bear trap variety, the French Ramy Securus. It works with any cable, but the release mechanism is reputed to freeze up;

and since it doesn't offer the flexibility of the Silvretta, would seem to be a second choice.

The more recent step-in touring bindings, although ingenious, cost more than the trusty cable binding and are less versatile. But they do offer some specialized advantages. If you plan a limited amount of touring in regular downhill ski boots, just for the sake of getting at untracked runs, these bindings are perfect as they are machined to withstand the leverage of stiff high-backed boots. If you are an expert skier who wants to ski challenging slopes in the back country (close to your limits of ability) these bindings will give you a greater safety factor through their multiple angles of release. And lastly, some are quickly adjustable to a great variety of boots. On a climb of Mt. McKinley, our party used skis equipped with the Swiss Su-Matic bindings; and with a few turns of a large thumb screw, we were able to use each other's skis interchangeably.

The Su-Matic is a traditional step-in heel unit that functions as a safety-release binding for downhill skiing. It moves up and down with the boot for climbing, pivoting on a pair of metal legs. It also locks in the raised-heel position, providing a flatter platform to stand on when walking straight up a slope.

In addition to the Su-Matic, leading step-in touring bindings are the Geze, the Marker *Haute Route* and some similar but rarely imported German bindings such as the ESS/Nevada combination. These all work on much the same principle: the heel is attached to a semi-flexible plastic strip running under the foot to the toe unit. This type of binding, although giving great lateral control, is not very adjustable to different size boots. They are quite safe, sometimes hard to find in shops, and cost from $50 to $75.

Unlike Nordic bindings, all Alpine touring bindings should be equipped with Arlberg straps or some other kind of anti-runaway safety strap. On Alpine terrain an unattached ski quickly becomes a lost ski.

POLES: Ski poles for Alpine touring are not very special. They should not be as long as Nordic poles, but frankly, any old ski poles will do, although they should be as light and well-balanced as possible. Aluminum downhill poles like Scott or Kerma are the ideal. The notion that one should replace the light downhill baskets with large leather and bamboo ones *à la* Army surplus is an absolute myth; they will only unbalance your skiing and catch on shrubs and branches. Solid plastic baskets are a help, however, as the poles don't sink so deeply into soft snow.

CLIMBING SKINS: Climbing on Alpine skis is accomplished by means of climbing skins. Originally these were made of seal skin, strapped or waxed onto the skis, and the backward-pointing hair prevented the skier from slipping back down the hill. Nowadays they are generally made of plush or mohair, which is cheaper, longer-lasting and just as effective. There are two main types: the Trima and Vinersa models.

Trima skins are attached to the skis by means of a series of pins, inserted permanently into the groove of the ski, which mate up with small metal plates on the skins themselves. Hence they commit you to use that one pair of skins with only that one pair of skis. But they are very neat and quick to put on and off, especially with cold fingers. And they have the added advantage of leaving the whole of the ski's edge exposed for side-stepping up hard crusty slopes.

They are becoming hard to find, however, as drilling holes in expensive fiberglass skis is not too popular. When you can find them, they cost about $20, plus possible installation charges.

The other type, the Vinersa, is attached by very simple metal clips and rubber bands, and can be freely changed from one set of skis to another, without drilling and preparing the skis. They cost around $20. Older model climbing skins which fasten with cloth straps are a source of potential frustration. The straps are easily cut through by the metal edges, and must be constantly repaired.

Worth mentioning are ski crampons or *harscheisen.* These ingenious metal teeth, which fasten to the skis just under the boots, look like one more gadget, but are in fact extremely useful. They were developed in the Alps for crossing steep, icy passes; and they permit one to zig-zag up a slope on skis where the only other mode of progress would be with crampons and ice axe. But they are a special tool for special places, and musn't be thought of as basic equipment, which comprises only the traditional gear: boots, skis, bindings and poles.

First steps

The goal of Alpine ski technique is not at all the same as that of Nordic skiing. Skiing on the level and climbing uphill are viewed as necessary and somewhat fatiguing, but above all simple aspects of the sport. They do not involve rhythm or balance, and are quickly learned. The real goal, and the real problem, is mastering the descent—the real pleasure as well, which amply compensates for the lost freedom of the Nordic skier's diagonal stride.

In this downhill-oriented world, there are appropriate turns and techniques for every level, beginner to expert. But the problem is always the same: how to turn, how to slow down, how to stop. For the beginner, another problem is: should I teach myself to ski, ask a friend to help me, or take lessons? This last alternative is an interesting one. For although the ski schools of major resorts are not oriented toward touring, the technique they teach is basically the same as that of the touring skier. The answer then is both yes and no.

Unfortunately, not all ski schools are staffed by competent instructors; not all ski schools teach a simplified functional modern technique. There is a whole generation of downhill skiers in America which still believes that the goal of ski technique is to look as pretty as possible—legs and skis glued together at any cost, shoulders and hips neatly tucked into an approved, stylized position. This kind of approach is a real dead end for the touring skier who must place function far ahead of form.

But if you know of a ski school with a progressive reputation for teaching movement rather than style, then go ahead and take lessons. They'll only speed your progress, especially at a ski school that stresses the GLM or 'graduated length method'—beginning on short (150 cm.) skis and graduating to normal length. Confide your interest in ski touring to your instructor and he may come up with some very special hints.

If there's no top ski school nearby, or if you plan to start out with friends, or just teach yourself, the following pages should help. (For the best detailed explanation of this subject, we can only refer you to George Joubert's excellent book, *Teach Yourself How to Ski*.)

BASICS: You can put on your equipment, we're certain, with no problems. Be sure your hands are correctly in the straps of your poles (see fig. 10). And start walking around. We hope you pick a flat area, surrounded by a few rather gentle slopes. Swinging your arms in a natural manner, you'll soon discover how helpful it is to plant your poles just behind your heels in order to keep from slipping back as you walk forward.

If you try to turn suddenly to one side, you will, of course, cross one ski over the other and fall. So take it easy. Using very small gentle steps, try what we call a star turn: leaving the tails of your skis in one place, start walking the tips around to the side, one at a time, like the hands of a

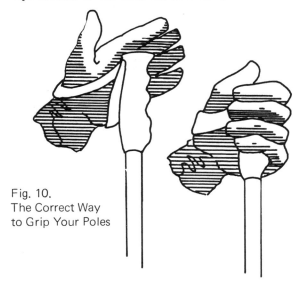

Fig. 10.
The Correct Way
to Grip Your Poles

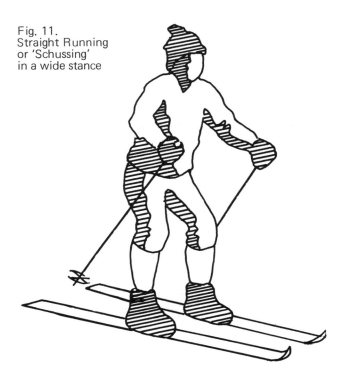

Fig. 11.
Straight Running
or 'Schussing'
in a wide stance

clock. You can also leave the tips of your skis in place and walk the tails around. Try that too.

But something tells you, after you've walked around for a while and turned this way and that, that these are only the preliminaries. When, you wonder, does the real skiing begin? For this you must climb to the top of a small rise.

The problem of climbing (of not sliding backward) is solved by *side-stepping* (see fig. 5 in chapter 2). Imagine that you are walking sideways up a staircase, and form the steps of that staircase by putting your skis solidly into the snow. If they are level you won't slide—up or down, backwards or forwards —and you can aid yourself with your poles as you climb.

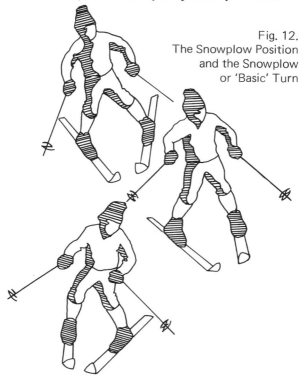

Fig. 12.
The Snowplow Position
and the Snowplow
or 'Basic' Turn

Having arrived at the summit of your mini-hill, turn to face the void. After a short, gentle slope, there should be a long flat or a slight uphill, so that you will come to a stop, even though you don't yet know how to stop on purpose. You are now ready to learn Alpine skiing's fundamental position: *the wide stance for downhill running.* Stand with your feet about as far apart as your hips are wide; flex a little at the ankles, knees and hips; spread your arms in front of you for lateral balance (like a tightrope walker); and, remembering to smile and breathe, push off with both poles and slide down the hill. The point of this wide-track stance is its great stability. Your balancing reflexes work from one foot to the other. And you absorb dips, bumps or rolls in the terrain by flexing, while your poles, like outriggers, are held ready to prevent any tipping over to the side (see fig. 11).

After a little of this *schussing* (straight sliding), you're ready to learn how to slow down, stop, and turn right and left. You'll do all this by means of the *snowplow* or 'wedge' position (see fig. 12). To snowplow, scrape out the tails of your skis by pushing your heels outward, but be careful not to cross the tips. Already you're going slower—the wider your snowplow, the slower you go. And by scraping out hard, and at the same time tilting your skis more onto their edge to increase the friction, you will come to a snowplow stop. It's much easier to snowplow with your stiffer boots than it is for the Nordic skier. But scraping out to a snowplow stop is still very difficult for loose-jointed people. In any case, it only works at very slow speeds. Otherwise you must turn out of the vertical or fall line to stop.

Turning is useful anyway, and it's done like this. Start out snowplowing straight down in a more or less narrow wedge, skis flat rather than edged (a gliding snowplow, not a braking snowplow). And then in order to turn right, *bend both knees forward and twist them slowly to the right, while pivoting your feet to the right in your boots.* You will slowly turn right (or left if that side was handier) and you will have become a skier. Earlier ski techniques stressed rotary or else counter-twisting movements of the shoulders and body, but you can forget all that; too much work for too little result. From here on, through expert skiing, you can remember this simple rule: *Turn with the feet and legs, balance with the arms and poles.* The body, of course, should be quiet and the head stable, to preserve a level visual horizon for better balance.

Practice your snowplow turns to both sides, concentrating on the steering action of feet and legs. Then start

Fig. 13.
The Traverse,
the flatter
the angle
—the slower
you go

linking them in small esses down the hill. By continuing to
turn, first across the hill, then slightly up, you will always
come to a stop. But if you want, you can straighten out
partway and *traverse* or ski diagonally down across the hill.
Traversing, at first, is just like skiing straight down. As you
traverse steeper slopes, you'll find that by pushing the
uphill (top) ski ahead about 6 inches, you can prevent your
ski tips from ever crossing. But don't make a big deal out of
traversing: stay relaxed, flexed, and remember to keep your
feet comfortably spread in a wide base. The angle of your
traverse (see fig. 13) determines your speed: shallow traverse,
slow; steeper traverse, faster. By connecting traverses with
snowplow turns, you can zig-zag slowly down easy hills.

By now you've learned a lot. This would be great progress for one day, or one weekend. You can now handle
beginner and easy intermediate slopes at most ski areas.
And you can go on an easy tour if the snow conditions
aren't too deep or difficult. If they are, you'll need one
more maneuver to make the corners of your zig-zag route
down the hill. It's the *kick turn*, done standing still (see
figure 3, in chapter 2).

CHRISTIES: These are the graceful, skidding turns used by
all accomplished skiers, intermediate to expert. The name is
a condensation of Christiania, a small town in Norway
where this type of turn was first done.

Our *basic turn*, the simple snowplow, can be easily
transformed into a *basic christie*. First, on a packed-out
slope, start into a snowplow turn from a traverse. Using
only a slight snowplow, try for a longer and rounder arc, at
somewhat faster speed. Now, just as your skis pass the
vertical (halfway around the turn), make a rapid, strong

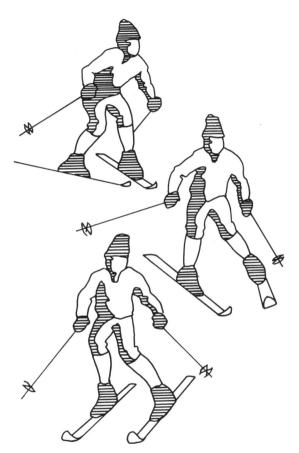

Fig. 14. The Basic Christie

pivoting effort with both feet and knees—trying to twist or pivot *both* skis into a sideways skid to complete the turn (see fig. 14). To succeed, you'll need both speed and determination, and a smoothly packed snow surface that offers a minimum of friction.

If you have trouble twisting both skis sideways into a skid from your gliding snowplow, then try it from a wide-track *schuss* straight down the hill. Start in a low crouch and with a little spring, decisively pivot both skis sideways into a skid which will bring you to a stop. We call this the *hockey stop*. Above all, don't imitate photos of expert skiers making christies with their skis held close together. The wide stance will be the key to your success. In it you are twice as stable, and anatomically your legs are twice as strong for pivoting, twisting and steering.

Once you've got your skis into a skid, you'll notice that they continue turning on their own. This is due to the *side camber* (or curve) cut into the ski, and its flex: the tip is the widest part and friction tends to slow it down, while the tails keep skidding, producing a turn. You can control this built-in turning action by continuing to steer the skidding skis with your feet, and the forward and inward push of your knees. After you've done your first christies, it's just a question of repetition and practice. But should you be unable to make a christie, it's time to take one or more lessons. The christie feeling is essential to any further progress.

Here's another hint. What you are really doing in the skidded or christie phase of the basic christie is sideslipping. You can practice this separately and it will help your christies. Stand across the hill on a short but steep pitch of packed snow while making your uphill edges bite into the snow with a little inward pressure of the ankles and knees. Now release that pressure, rolling ankles and knees slightly down the hill, letting your skis flatten on the slope—you will begin to slide sideways, or sideslip (see fig. 15). To stop, just re-edge your skis as before, keeping your balance with your poles. With a little practice, you will learn to control your sideslips both down and across the hill. As your skis sideslip there is less friction, so that by applying steering you easily get a christie: try steering your tips uphill to stop. Your basic christie will be much improved. You can also sideslip down pitches too steep for you to ski directly.

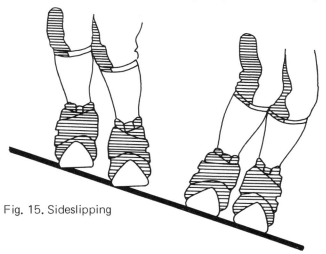

Fig. 15. Sideslipping

What about unpacked snow? It's much harder to make the skis skid because of increased resistance, so we suggest a simple form of *unweighting*. As you steer your *stemmed* (snowplowed) skis down the hill toward the fall line, hold your pole a little forward, ready to plant. (Right turn, right pole; left turn, left pole.) In the fall line, plant your pole in the snow; and, supporting yourself on it, jump both skis sideways, landing with very bent knees to absorb the shock. The jump will free your skis from the snow and should bring you around, although one can never skid as freely in deep snow as on the pack.

You are now an intermediate or christie skier. Of course, there is a variety of possible christies, and we haven't even mentioned the advanced forms. Our basic christie is a close cousin of the old stem christie, a complicated turn that stressed unweighting, shifting weight from ski to ski, closing the skis to a tight parallel position at the end, and various other body movements. Fortunately, the simplified basic christie works just as well, and is replacing the stem christie in progressive ski schools.

One more comment. Weight shift (stepping to the outside ski of a turn) has been a part of nearly all skiing systems. We don't stress it for two reasons. First, it will occur naturally, due to centrifugal force, the sharper the turn and the higher the speed. Second, in powder or any deep snow, the skier must preserve *equal* weighting so that one ski doesn't bury itself beneath the surface. So why acquire habits you must unlearn later? From the start, *try to use both legs independently but equally.*

SPECIAL TOURING TECHNIQUES: The obvious subject here is the use of climbing skins on the level and uphill portions of a tour, but frankly there's almost nothing to it. A few suggestions will suffice. First, make sure the straps which cinch up the skins to the undersides of the ski tips are tight and secured. If they loosen up, you won't know it at first, but will have more and more difficulty gripping. Skins will generally adhere on steeper slopes than will Nordic climbing waxes, but there is a limit. A few moments experimenting on a steep hillside, and you will discover this limit for a given snow condition. Somewhere before you reach this limit, it's more practical and a lot less tiring, to give up the straight ascent and begin zig-zagging up the hill with long traverses linked by kick-turns. By unlacing or loosening the topmost laces of your boots, you can obtain greater ankle bend. This makes it easier to stand solidly and flat-footed, rather than back on your heels, while climbing a steep slope. When your skins start sliding back a little before gripping, lift the whole ski and set it down smartly in the snow, instead of shuffling it forward on the surface. But this means you're approaching the limits of adherence. Also, don't rely on your arms and back pressure with the poles to keep from slipping: always choose a shallower angle of traverse.

And what of the descent? Regrettably, the *full* pleasure of Alpine-style touring is only open to the expert or advanced skier (see next section)—and you've got a ways to go. Certain conditions are particularly easy for beginners and intermediates: light new powder (less than a foot) over a settled base; settled and crusted snow where the skier doesn't break through; and spring or corn snow, a granular surface that varies from frozen to several inches of slush, but is invariably easy to ski on. These surfaces are just as easy to turn on with simple christies as the machine-groomed practice slopes of a ski area. Deep new snow, soft sticky snow, light breakable crust and unevenly drifted snow are all quite difficult. And frankly, the novice Alpine skier doesn't have a chance of skiing gracefully downhill in such conditions. Paradoxically, ice is quite easy for the beginner to turn on; it feels awkward but the skis skid easily. Of course, the novice should avoid steep icy slopes at any cost, as once he falls, he is not likely to stop until he meets a tree or rock at the bottom of the slope.

In the difficult conditions mentioned above, you can still enjoy touring; just 'cool it' on the downhill stretches. Descend with long shallow traverses and kick-turns, just as you went up. Nordic skiers do it all the time.

In deep powder you will feel out of your element, but you will have one unexpected advantage. The friction of so much snow slows you down to the point that you can ski directly down much steeper slopes than usual without gaining much speed. In deep powder, snowplow turns will work only at very, very slow speeds. And if things are going well, you can try the jumped version of the basic christie described above. With a pack, of course, everything becomes harder, which is another reason for prudent descents at this stage.

We haven't said anything about falls so far, assuming that you will fall down quite regularly as you learn, and somehow pick yourself up. Ski instructors have invented some fantastically complex methods to help unathletic people get back on their feet. Obviously one uses his poles to stand up with, but anyone who really has trouble getting up from a fall is probably not in good enough physical shape to consider ski touring.

Much more important, especially in the difficult and potentially dangerous conditions we've just mentioned, is learning to fall safely. The safest and most painless falls are backwards and into the hill; in other words, sitting down, the way your legs naturally bend. When things get scary, it's no disgrace to 'bail out' by sitting back and down. There are, however, a number of dangerous ways one should *not* fall. Forward falls are generally bad. These happen either from burying one's ski tips in a dip or gully, or from inadvertently doing the splits—you watch paralyzed as your ski tips slowly, inexorably diverge. To avoid the first case, try to ride into dips with your weight on your heels, maybe advancing one ski tip as a kind of antenna. In the second case, throw yourself quickly to one side or the other, as it's usually impossible to pull your skis back together once they have begun to split. Also, attempt to land on your side and hip when you fall. Trying to break the fall with your knee is just asking for a sprain or pulled ligament. And lastly, if you are using safety bindings, don't be surprised if your skis don't release at every fall. Well-adjusted bindings will only come off under slow, steady, bone-breaking torsion.

But enough gloom. Alpine skiing, we hope you've found out, is not really that difficult. It is certainly more involved in the number and complexity of maneuvers than its Nordic counterpart, and for this reason, seldom becomes as instinctive. By now, though, you should have experienced the special thrills of skiing down, letting your tracks stretch out behind you. In the next section, we'll see where it all leads.

Advanced technique

What are the goals of advanced Alpine technique? For the downhill-only skier there are many, but for our purposes we have selected one: complete freedom of movement in deep and challenging snow. We've seen that making a con-

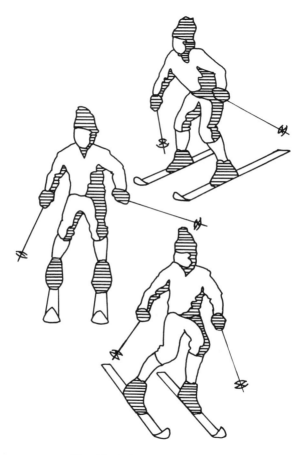

Fig. 16. A Simple Parallel Turn

trolled, fluid descent over a hard, smooth, snow surface is fairly easy. But in deep powder even most so-called advanced skiers are stumped; they make a few turns, flounder and fall. Yet one who has mastered powder invariably claims that it's easier than the big icy bumps or moguls encountered on packed slopes. What then is the secret?

PARALLEL SKIING: The traditional reason for making parallel turns has been to look elegant on the slope; this is nonsense. A parallel turn is not one with the two skis glued together, but rather a turn in which both skis do the same thing at the same time, as a result of parallel turning efforts exerted by each leg. Once mastered, it is generally the simplest, most functional, and doubtless the most graceful way to turn the skis. By turning, of course, we both change direction and control our speed; it is the turn that conquers the slope. And the only turn that really works in deep powder is a parallel turn.

A simple parallel turn happens almost automatically. If we continue to practice basic christies, we will depend less and less on the snowplow or stem opening to start the turn. The steered skid of both skis will start earlier in the turn; and finally we will be starting the turn by a simple vigorous twist of both feet and both bent legs—a simple rudimentary parallel turn. In other words, just as the basic turn (snowplow) evolved into the basic christie (old stem christie), so the basic christie evolves naturally into a simple parallel christie, if we do it faster and more aggressively. (See fig. 16). But to go beyond this start, there are several principles which can turn this simple parallel skid into a nearly universal turn. We've already discussed the stability of a wide stance, and using the increased leverage of bent knees and feet to turn

Fig. 17. An Advanced Parallel Turn

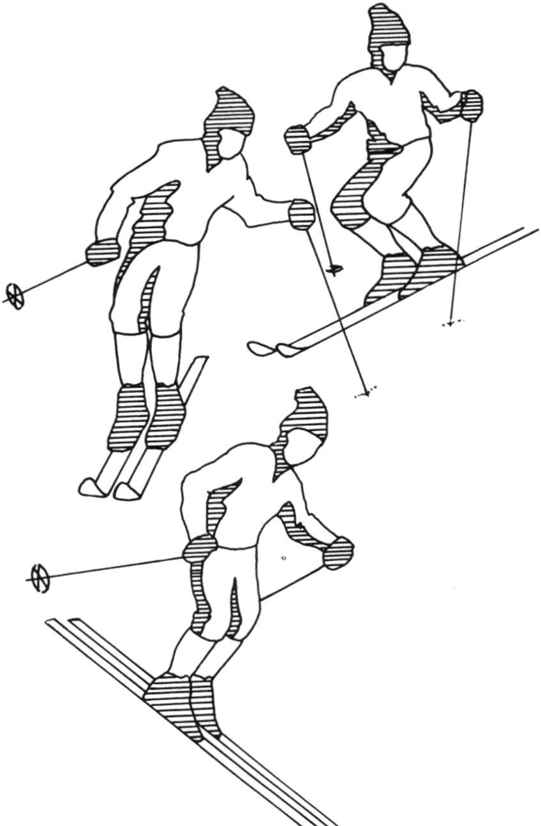

the skis *beneath* the mass of the trunk. The next point is *unweighting*.

Unweighting is anything the skier does to reduce the friction between skis and snow. This is much more important in the wilderness than at a ski area, for on packed slopes there is really very little friction to keep the skis from turning, especially at moderate to high speed. In a way, unweighting replaces speed, which can mean greater safety for the touring skier in difficult conditions. The most common form of unweighting, *up-unweighting*, is an upward spring from a preparatory crouched position. The skier thinks of projecting his center of gravity (his hips) away from the ground by the rapid extension of his bent legs. (You can try it on a bathroom scale and watch the needle drop.) It's not even necessary to leave the ground, although this creates total unweighting. And if one wishes to prolong the moment of reduced weight, just follow the extension with a smooth folding or flexion. During this instant of unweighting, the skis can be easily swiveled down the hill into the new turn. The only requirement for this kind of unweighting is to prepare for the turn by sinking to a low position from which to spring up. Generally, planting your pole will trigger this *up* movement. There are several other forms of unweighting, by sudden kneeling and by rebounding off one's edges, but these are more applicable to packed and icy slopes than to deep snow.

The next key element in advanced parallel skiing is *anticipation*. In a specific sense, anticipation means swiveling your upper body (shoulders to hips) down the hill, in the direction of the coming turn, just before turning. The idea is simple. Upper body and legs tend to line up the same way, so that as soon as the skis stop gripping the snow (unweighting), both legs and skis tend to 'unwind' or 'uncoil' themselves to point downhill in line with the pre-twisted mass of the body. (The skier's trunk is heavier, thus more stable; and anyway, the planted pole keeps the body from 'unwinding' back in the direction of the skis.)

Anticipation thus adds a tremendously strong passive tendency-to-turn to any pivoting efforts you make with your muscles. You are like a torsion bar untwisting, and your turns will be twice as strong—or twice as easy.

The simplest way to get into this useful position of anticipation prior to turning, is by doing a *counter turn*. A counter turn is a small uphill christie just before turning downhill. To do a counter turn, you sink slightly and steer uphill with feet and knees, *but without turning your body*. Thus you wind up still facing the original traverse, that is, with your upper body facing across your skis in a position of anticipation. At the end of this counter turn, plant your downhill pole and, supporting yourself on it, rise up and forward into the turn (unweighting). You will feel your skis pivot back under the axis of your body which faces more or less down the hill. The turn once started is steered like any other, with pressure from feet and knees, which are once more bent after the initial extension.

Sound complicated? Not at all. What we've just described is an *advanced parallel turn*, using both anticipation and up-unweighting. The counter turn is the preparation for both elements: sinking preparatory to springing up, and winding the body up against itself in preparation for the 'unwinding' movement initiating the turn. Study figure 17 for a graphic picture of this turn. Once mastered it is tremendously easy to do, and can be done in virtually all conditions.

One more point. It's not necessary to do a counter turn before each advanced parallel turn. The tail end of one turn can serve perfectly as the counter turn for the following one. The compression experienced from deceleration in the last third of every downhill turn, actually aids the skier in preparing his extension or *up* for the next turn. The anticipation is obtained by keeping the body facing more-or-less always down the hill, not across, while feet and skis turn back and forth beneath the trunk. This anticipation is not significant in sweeping long-radius turns, but is very helpful in medium-sized turns, and absolutely essential in linking small turns down the hill (*wedeln*).

Nor is this turn the only advanced parallel turn. There is a whole family of them, but they all start from a counter turn and use some form of unweighting. Most of these, rebound turns and jet *christies*, the sliding jet turn or the Joubert "S" turn, are more applicable to hard snow and man-made bumps than to soft snow. Yet one principle is the same in all: the skier uses energy stored in the preparation, or counter turn, to make the start of the turn easier. An expert skier often feels he is *letting* his skis turn downhill, not forcing them to turn. Obviously, our advanced turn works in powder, but learning to do it there is another story.

DEEP SNOW: The initial problems in mastering powder are psychological, but they are still real. Deep snow feels spooky—you're no longer standing on something solid, and there is an erie, slow-motion feeling as though you were skiing in fluffy white glue. This is due to the increased lateral resistance of the snow. You ski through it, not on it, and any jerky movements or sudden turns are doomed to failure, since you run up against a wall of compressed snow (in skiing jargon you 'catch an edge') and you fall. All this takes getting used to, but there is a method.

The rule in deep powder is: *stability before technique.* You have to stay on your feet no matter what. To gain this necessary stability we must do two things. We'll modify our stance slightly—lower, more flexed than usual, arms extended wide for balance, and weight rigorously even on the two skis. Avoid really sitting back, but stand flat-footed with a little extra weight on the heels. Next, we have to do a lot of straight running, first in long shallow traverses, which will

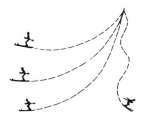

Fig. 18.
The Fan Pattern, an excercise for mastering powder snow

gradually steepen as we practice uphill christies in what's called a fan pattern (see fig. 18). Our skis won't sideslip through so much snow, so to turn uphill to a stop, we must sink very low and 'grind' the tails of our skis down into the

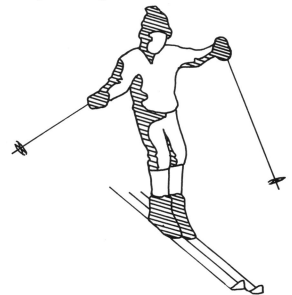

Fig. 19. The Start of a Long-radius Turn in Powder

snow. This produces a slow uphill turn. Be patient, you really will stop eventually. It's important to learn to stop with these wide 'pull-out' christies, because someday you'll start a turn and suddenly find yourself stuck in the fall line, gathering speed. This is an anti freak-out exercise. Once you can slowly turn out of a vertical schuss in deep powder, your confidence will increase tenfold.

Now you're ready to try a complete downhill turn. Remember the friction of the snow is holding you back, so start from a steep traverse, close to the fall line. For the moment, forget your counter turn. After gaining some speed, sink down, weight even, downhill pole ready. Planting your pole, rise straight up off both feet, lifting your outside hand above your shoulder to accentuate this unweighting and tilt you to the inside of the turn. At the same time make an effort to pivot your skis toward the fall line, while thrusting them ahead of you. If all goes well, you will have started a long-radius turn, your skis will be banked against the snow, and you can complete the turn by sinking down and pressing the tails into the snow. (See fig. 19.)

Once again, it sounds complicated but it's not. This type of turn is often called a *light christie*, and the skier feels as if he is floating into the fall line. After you have succeeded with one, try several more singly, skiing each to a stop. Then, link alternate turns with short traverses to provide a breathing space. And finally, link consecutive turns—the sinking, at the end of one, preparing you to spring up to start the next.

Once you've got the hang of it, go back to counter turns with anticipation, and they will help you shorten the radius of your turns. The counter turn is invaluable. It gives a kind of preview of the snow you will encounter during the turn, it sets up a feeling of rhythm before the turn, and seems to force one into the downhill plunge with a minimum of hesitation.

Paradoxically, the single medium-to-long-radius turn (just described) is not the easiest turn to do in deep powder, but it is the easiest to learn. Technically, *wedeln* (short linked turns down the fall line) is far easier, because each turn is a kind of dynamic recovery from any possible loss of balance in the previous one. But the balance you acquire in long turns will stand you in good stead; and at first, there's too much to think about to hope to succeed with small linked turns.

Anticipation is the key to fall-line skiing. Remain facing downhill as you try for shorter, linked turns, and grind the tails of your skis into the snow, first on one side then the other. As you use more anticipation you will use less *up* movement, and finally the *up* will be replaced by a kind of relaxation of legs and thighs as you feel pressure build up underfoot at the end of a turn. Relaxing, you let this pressure push your ski tips up and out; you pivot them to the other side and once more press your heels down, to create another invisible 'pressure bump' to turn upon: your body hardly moves; you have become a master of deep snow.

There are a few powder myths to dispose of, before we go on to really bad snow conditions. One of the most wide-spread is that the skis must be held flat, to slice sideways through the snow. The opposite is true. In fact, flattened skis cause the most common type of powder fall, catching an outside edge and falling over downhill. Good powder skiers *bank* their skis, so that pressure against the whole bottom of the ski pushes them into the turn. Raising the outside arm as you start the turn is a good trick to accomplish this; you'll see it in almost all photos of good powder skiers.

Another myth is that the skis must be held side by side like a mono-ski. This idea makes more sense in deep snow than anywhere else, but even so a lot of the best skiers don't do it. Find out what is comfortable for you. There is admittedly danger that your skis will track in different directions; or, unequally weighted, one may dive and one float, if they aren't held closely together. But you can pivot more powerfully from a wider stance. In any case, avoid the true wide track in favor of a semi-wide, or even a narrow stance for deep snow.

The final powder myth is that one must sit way back on the tails of the skis to make the tips plane up out of the snow—or adopt a very low position, as if seated in an invisible chair, which comes to the same thing. This extreme position was once the sign of the true powder hound, someone who had mastered the exotic Alta technique. Modern powder skiers adopt a more moderate stance, weighting their heels only enough so that the ski tips don't dive, adjusting their stance to the type of snow, steepness of slope and their speed. The seated position on the tails *does* give tremendous twisting leverage over the skis; but as it restricts the free play of the legs, we suggest you keep this position in reserve for *really* deep and *exceptionally* heavy powder.

SPECIAL CONDITIONS: Certain snow conditions are particularly difficult and challenging to ski in. We'll cover several common problem types and the methods used to handle them. The general categories are: heavy snow, drifted snow, crusty snow and, in a separate sense, ice.

By 'heavy snow' we mean wet, deep, new snow that has begun to set up in the sun, often encountered in spring, known in the Rockies as 'California powder' and in California as 'Sierra cement.' To ski this troublesome stuff, we take the same approach as for powder with the following differences.

First, more unweighting: the more the snow grips your skis, the more you must spring up to free them from this grip at the start of the turn. Often, in bad snow, this means jumping the skis completely out of the snow to start the turn. The problem with this 'leap and land' technique is the landing. If you pivot your skis too far and land cross-wise to your original direction, you will come to a jarring stop and doubtless crash in the heavy snow. Likewise, if you land with stiff legs. But it can be done. In fact, in extremely heavy sticky snow you may have to unweight several times, or hop several times to get all the way around. One way to prolong the unweighted period after your strong *up* motion, is to follow it with a so-called *avalement* movement. This is a rapid jack-knifing or upward folding of the thighs against the body, first used by French racers and later adapted by experts to both packed slopes and deep snow. This exaggerated second-phase folding also cushions the landing, if your extension lifts you completely off the

Fig. 20. A Turn for Very Bad Snow

snow. (For a clearer picture, see the drawing of a turn for very bad snow, fig. 20.)

Along with strong unweighting, we suggest skiing a good deal slower than normal. This is safer as your skis could be trapped in an awkward dangerous position by heavy snow; and the unweighting will replace momentum. Also, use your poles a good deal more than normal to preserve your balance. Especially the outside pole which can be planted several times in the course of one turn, like pawing the ground with a crutch or outrigger.

The problem with wind-drifted snow is its variability. The skier is suddenly decelerated by hitting a dense drift; or he may suddenly shoot forward as his skis slide on top of a section of hard wind-slab. If you feel your skis digging in or slowing down, shift your weight to the heels by collapsing your legs, and throw your arms and poles out sideways ready to prop yourself up. Then as your skis slow or stop, your center of gravity (temporarily behind your feet) will be thrown forward to a more or less normal position. Do the same thing in powder, if you feel yourself hit heavier or deeper snow. If your skis shoot out in front of you, you can catch up by throwing your arms ahead of you. Remember: *control your skis with your legs, balance with your arms.*

Of course, wind-drifted snow may also have a thin, brittle crust formed by the wind. Skiing this is like skiing any crusted snow. Crust forms on snow as a result of wind action, settling with temperature change, and the thawing and freezing that will eventually form spring or corn snow. If the crust is solid enough to bear the skier's weight, there's no problem, but so-called *breakable crust* is the skier's nightmare. If the crust is just on the verge of breaking under your weight, you can use the counter turn as a sort of test. If the snow doesn't give under the pressure of the counter turn, the actual downhill turn should work fine. Conversely, if you can't even do a counter turn, you won't have a chance of turning downhill. So pick yourself up, and resign yourself to a series of kick turns till you reach more hospitable snow.

Extremely strong skiers *can* ski breakable crust that breaks at every move (dropping them into the softer snow beneath) by using the 'leap and land' technique. But even the strongest are afraid of it, and to keep their speed as low as possible, generally do a series of linked jumped turns straight down the fall line. The best skiers would seldom try it when wearing a pack. A fast traverse can be very dangerous in breakable crust. For often, with one's skis trapped beneath the heavy crust, it's even impossible to make an uphill turn to stop. The skier must bail out and sit down to stop, and this could have serious consequences. So, unless you spend all winter on skis practicing such things, ski very carefully in breakable crust.

Our last problem, ice, is nearly insoluble with Alpine touring equipment. Positive control on icy slopes demands fiberglass skis, sharpened edges, and above all, high stiff boots. On low-angled slopes, things aren't too bad. You will, of course, feel insecure, but the solution is to spread your feet for stability, *angulate* or push your ankles and knees into the hill to help your edges grip, and grin and bear it. It's rare to find a whole slope or a whole mountain covered with real ice. The touring skier should definitely avoid skiing down steep icy slopes if he isn't wearing stiff downhill boots (and he usually isn't).

On a ski expedition up the west buttress of Mt. McKinley, we had to leave our skis at the 15,000-foot level when we encountered a slope of steep blue ice. Two of the best skiers in the country, Wally Rothgab and Dick Dorworth, member and coach, respectively, of the national Alpine racing squad, and both brilliant skiers on ice, were with us and judged it absolutely impossible with our equipment. (Double boots, step-in bindings, and Kneisel G.S. skis.)

Climbing icy slopes with ski crampons is not particularly dangerous, but remember you have to come down. If you are descending an icy slope and the steepness makes you hesitate to try a turn, above all, *do not kick turn*. Should you slip and fall in the spread-eagled position, there is absolutely no way to right yourself or stop until you hit something. Far better to sideslip down the entire slope facing the same way.

And on the subject of falls, a last word of advice. Try to get in the habit of reacting fast. Relax and hit softly, but *immediately* get your skis beneath you, hit your edges, and push yourself back on your feet. Do this even when you don't need to. Top skiers survive fantastic falls on steep dangerous slopes because of their habit of getting back on their feet almost before they've stopped falling.

One last problem is roped skiing on a crevassed glacier, but we'll cover this under mountaineering in chapter 10.

So now we can all ski, one way or the other: beginner, intermediate, or master, Alpine style or Nordic. Now, we're through looking at ski technique by itself, and in the following chapters we'll look at the context in which we do it: *the ski tour*, long or short, and all that goes with it.

4. The One-Day Ski Tour

So far, we have been concerned exclusively with the *how* of skiing: its movements, its specialized techniques, and special ski equipment. Obviously, from your first hesitant steps to a real mastery of skiing, you will have to pay a lot of dues. This apprenticeship is not in itself painful, but we hope you don't wait until you're an advanced skier before venturing on your first tours. These need not be long, strenuous or difficult to organize. But unless you get away from your practice area, from any well-known slopes, you will not have experienced the real flavor of wilderness skiing. It is not skiing on cross-country skis that gives one this feeling, but skiing cross country.

The one-day ski tour is the ideal introduction to wilderness skiing. We can't recommend too strongly that you make quite a few short tours, until you feel at home on untracked snow, on an unmarked trail, before launching out on your first overnight or multi-day venture. A one-day tour is usually more of a *skiing adventure* than longer tours, because with light packs (or no packs) one can ski at a higher standard, and therefore attempt runs or cover terrain that would be too challenging for the skier burdened down with food, stoves, tents, or, as Zorba put it, the full catastrophe.

The specific problems of a one-day ski tour are staying warm and comfortable on the trail; not getting lost; exercising a certain judgment in the choice of a route suitable for the party's strength and skiing ability; and being prepared to cope with the minor emergencies that may come up; broken equipment, accidents and injuries, or an unexpected night out. We will cover these areas under the heading:

Fig. 21.
The Well-dressed Ski Tourer

clothes and other equipment (about which we've said nothing so far), *planning the tour* and *on the trail* (skiing strategy for a one-day tour).

Clothes and other equipment

Despite what advertising copy in the skiing magazines would have you believe, the downhill skier dresses first for fashion, then for function. For the wilderness skier, it's the opposite: function above all. For us, function means both comfort and protection. (One generally thinks of protection from cold and driving winds, but in spring, excess heat and blistering sun can be the main problem.)

There are a few general principles of functional dress. The most important is that insulation is proportional to thickness (often merely thickness of trapped air) and not to weight. A fine principle indeed. It lets us realize certain other *desiderata*: lightest possible weight, adequate ventilation, and a variety of layers so that one can tailor his dress to the needs of the moment—adding or shedding a windproof outer layer, choosing a slightly warmer, or a much warmer insulating combination according to the demands of exertion and weather.

The most important natural materials for mountain clothing are down, for its lightness and compressibility, and wool which insulates well, even when wet. But nylon and synthetic materials have become justly popular for their great strength and light weight, and should be used wherever practical.

The Nordic skier on a day tour will tend to dress a little lighter than his Alpine counterpart, as his stride generates more body heat while moving, but he can get just as chilled during a long lunch stop. Basically the same gear is appropriate for both. So, assuming the existence of a hypothetical 'average touring skier,' let's see how he's dressed, from inside out, from head to foot.

INNER GARMENTS: Long underwear is a subject of controversy. Some skiers never do without, even on mild days; others never use long underwear on the theory that it's better to add removable outer layers like wind pants when it's really cold. The two authors of this book, in fact, belong to opposing camps, so it's something you'll have to decide on the basis of personal experience. In really cold conditions long underwear can be invaluable, but annoying to take off on the trail. Avoid scratchy, pure wool longs which are irritating as you walk and ski.

Sometimes ski touring seems like an endless struggle between too much and too little heat. A practical solution to reduce the number of clothing changes is the Norwegian-type string or fishnet undershirt, which works both to ventilate and insulate the body. Long underpants of string material are also available and make a good substitute for wool/cotton ones.

Wool shirts also have their staunch proponents, but some find them too heavy for the movements required in active skiing. The standard skier's turtle neck of cotton knit is hard to beat, and can be combined with a nylon windshirt for comfortable skiing in a slight breeze. These nylon windshirts (also a standard downhill skier's item) weigh almost nothing and are invaluable. Although it contradicts theory and logic, wearing a windshirt *under* a ski sweater seems to double the warmth of the sweater.

The touring skier prefers knickers to long trousers or

tight-fitting stretch pants. They permit greater freedom of movement, and after a bout with wet or soggy snow, he can change into dry socks rather than dry pants. Material for knickers, and indeed all outer garments, should be a smooth, tightly-woven fabric, for wind resistance and impermeability to snow. Knickers that are too baggy tend to catch snow, but they should be loose and comfortable. Good tight knickers of elastic stretch fabric are okay. These are very wind and snow resistant, and have become popular in Europe both for ski touring and ice climbing in the Alps, but are in short supply here.

Another good knicker resembles old-time baggy ski pants, and can fasten both at the ankle and at the knee. These are easy to make out of old ski pants (pre-1960's), by cutting off the foot stirrups and adding the knicker cuff. A velcro-tape band is ideal for the closing, but be careful to keep it free of powder snow, which clogs the tiny 'teeth.' Shorter, knee-length knickers of light poplin are preferred by Nordic skiers, while wool/synthetic blends give greater warmth and durability for Alpine-style touring, among high peaks with some climbing.

Whatever your style of knicker—and it goes without saying that there no rules: you can ski tour in a pair of old jeans if you wish—they are always worn with long socks. Here again a wool/synthetic blend is ideal. Some of the most practical socks rise above the knee to avoid the common 'knicker gap' of cold skin; and a sock that has some elastic throughout is preferable to a single elastic band at the top. So-called 'thermal' socks, which have a soft lining like Terry-cloth and seem to cushion the foot, are very popular ski socks in a normal short length, and if you look hard you can find them in knicker length too.

Most touring skiers prefer two pairs of socks, one knee-length and one regular. Some control over the skis is sacrificed, but then, touring boots aren't the last word in control either. More important, there is less likelihood of blisters and foot problems and, of course, the feet are warmer.

OUTER GARMENTS: With knickers, one is generally obliged to wear gaiters. These are nylon or cotton tubes (fastened to the boot with an elastic cuff and straps or cords) which rise up the leg to keep snow from sticking and melting on the socks, or getting into the boots. In deep snow, ankle-high gaiters are useless, and we recommend knee-high gaiters with an adjustable closing on top. In a couple of inches of new snow, or on a hard surface, you won't need gaiters, nor do you need them for Nordic skiing in a track. Really good gaiters were hard to find a few years ago, but now there is a great variety. The best ones are made of heavy nylon duck, have a full-length heavy gauge nylon zipper, and should fit *your* boots snugly. All zippers (on jackets and packs as well) should have large tabs for easy use with cold or mittened hands. You can make these easily. And watch out for the tiny teeth of small-gauge zippers: they will break if you look at them wrong.

The insulation layers are rounded out by a wool ski sweater and/or a light down jacket or down sweater. Any old sweater will do, but a dense (not necessarily thick) knit is warmer in windy conditions, and less likely to pick up a crust of powder when you fall. The French Montant sweaters are almost ideal.

Down jackets have long since won acceptance by mountaineers; they are the lightest, warmest garments available.

It's often said, however, that they are too warm for ski touring. We disagree. The lightweight, sewn-through 'down sweater' is probably still too warm for wear on the trail except in the vilest weather. But considering that its weight and bulk in the pack (well stuffed in a small sack) is less than half that of a heavy sweater, it's obviously very practical. Until it gets wet, that is. Then the down balls up, and it's about as warm as a wet tee shirt. For this reason experienced mountain travelers keep their down jackets safely in the waterproof stuff-sack when it's raining or drizzling (yes, it sometimes rains on a ski tour). A good compromise is to take both a down sweater and a medium-weight ski sweater.

The wind parka, sometimes used with wind pants, is the outer, protective shell of the wilderness skier's outfit. These protective outer parkas are made in a variety of fabrics: nylon, cotton, and blends, as well as polyurethane-coated, waterproof fabrics. The waterproof climber's parka or *cagoule* is definitely *not* recommended; if worn on the trail in freezing temperatures, a coating of ice will form on the inside from condensation. (In warm, spring conditions in the West, a *cagoule* would be okay.) Nylon seems preferable; a nylon parka can be doubled, making it much more windproof, and still weigh less than poplin or 'ventile cloth' models.

The parka should be large enough to fit loosely over all your clothes, including the down sweater, and should extend below the hips. A 'crotch strap' can keep the parka from riding up in bad weather. Make sure that the hood is large enough to go over a knit ski hat without constricting your movement when wearing a pack. The pull-over type is a little warmer, but the front-zipper model can be unzipped for ventilation. You can't have too many pockets, although a large 'kangaroo pouch' pocket will do. If the parka is doubled, a zipper giving access to the back 'compartment' creates an immense pocket which is handy if you don't carry a pack.

Wind pants are something of an unnecessary luxury in most circumstances, except in deep powder, since knickers and gaiters are quite windproof. There is a French parka/pants combination, much beloved by powder skiers who have been able to get one, in which both pants and parka are stowed away in the parka pocket, (turned inside out to form a small 'fanny' pack that ties around the waist). More pull-over parkas should have this feature, which only involves a two-sided zipper and two cloth tapes sewn to the inside of the 'kangaroo' pocket.

ACCESSORIES: Our well-dressed wilderness skier is finished off with gloves, a hat, dark glasses, and the necessary goop to keep his face and lips from burning to a crisp in the reflected sunlight. For day-touring no ultra-specialized protective gear is needed, since generally one doesn't go touring in bad weather. On a longer trip, of course, one may be overtaken by bad weather, and even obliged to travel in it for several days.

Ordinary leather ski gloves work fine; most are insulated with foam. But on longer trips, with the possibility of severe conditions, we would suggest mitts, either of down-filled nylon, or the astonishingly warm raw-wool mitts from Dachstein, Austria, that are the world standard for ice and winter climbing. These latter can be used with impermeable nylon overmitts, or by themselves, as loose snow merely forms an insulating icy crust on the mitt. Silk or nylon inner gloves could be a help, especially in cold-weather photography, or while fiddling with jammed bindings and frozen climbing skins.

Likewise with goggles and dark glasses: the simplest will suffice for a day tour. Dark glasses are more comfortable than goggles, and preferable in most circumstances. For high-altitude, ski glasses are available with leather side-pieces to cut glare. But even on the highest glaciers, most people eventually cut these off and throw them away as they make one sweat too much.

Goggles, however, are preferable to glasses in deep powder skiing, and in storms and blizzards. Here only the best will do. Cheap goggles fog up and are the source of endless frustration. Good ones have a two-layer lens with a sealed, dead-air space between; consequently the outer lens stay cold, and inner lens warm, without the usual condensation. The Smith goggle, invented by a famous Utah powder skier, was the first of these, although now there are several similar models. Their only disadvantage is the price, around $20. It seems like a fortune, but when you need them nothing else will work; in fact skiing deep powder without this kind of goggle is like skiing half blind. The $20 we spent on these goggles three years ago is the best ski equipment buy we've ever made.

Knitted ski hats are a good expression of a skier's whimsy and color preference. Balaclava helmets are only for storms and wind; and, even then, a silk scarf or bandana covering the lower half of your face does just as well. On spring tours, especially at high altitudes, a hat with a brim is a near essential, as is some kind of opaque, total block sun cream. More tours are ruined by forgetting the seemingly trivial tubes of sun cream and lip protector than by any other cause.

PACKS: Even if you do need all the clothing we've just mentioned, you won't wear it all at once. To carry spare items—sweater, parka, lunch, a small emergency and repair kit, a camera, whatever—you will want a light rucksack with a few special features.

The pack should be made of waterproof nylon, as you may wind up sitting on it in the snow. It should have a

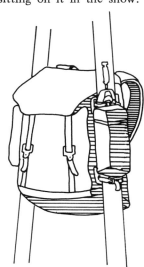

Fig. 22.
A Light
Touring
Pack with
Skis
Attached

waistband to prevent it from flopping around when you're skiing fast. You can easily improvise a waist strap on a pack you've already got, with a couple of pieces of nylon sling. Ideally, it should have ski straps on the sides. These are for carrying your skis when you have to walk some distance to the snow line, or if frozen morning crust makes it faster to start the tour on foot. Sometimes, instead of ski straps, side pockets are attached in such a way that the skis can be thrust down between them and the pack itself (the bindings keep them from sliding too far). Once attached to the pack, the skis should be tied together at the tips, forming a large 'A,' so that the tails of the skis don't bang you in the shins at every step. This method of carrying the skis vertically, on the sides of the pack, is perfect for walking in forested terrain. But above timberline, with no obstacles on either side, we've found it more convenient to carry the skis horizontally, tied crosswise on the top of the pack.

Many packs sold with the label 'ski mountaineering pack' are not really very suitable, being short and lumpy, and almost invariably too small. Even on a one-day tour, a large pack half-full is more comfortable than a small pack stuffed to bursting. Rucksacks made in Germany have an interesting feature found in no others: a foam-padded back. But once again, you don't need the best to go touring; with a little experience, you will discover just what your own requirements are.

A small canvas or nylon 'fanny' pack is ideal for carrying a snack and a few odds and ends on a very short tour—half a day, for example, where you know the route and the conditions well, and there is little likelihood of the unexpected. Of course, there's no reason why you have to take a pack at all, if you're just going skiing for a few hours, especially if it's a short excursion with the idea of skiing down a technically difficult slope or couloir.

ODDS AND ENDS: Aside from lunch and something to drink, consider taking the following.

A small repair kit with certain indispensable items. For Nordic skis, a spare plastic ski tip is extremely light, and will save the day if you should hit a tree stump and splinter the tip of your ski. (Metal and fiberglass skis are so strong that a broken tip is almost unheard of.) For Alpine skiers, a spare cable for the bindings and an ingenious combination tool—screw driver, wrench, pliers and wire-cutter in one—are the key items. A small coil of soft wire and a roll of adhesive tape can repair everything from torn ski pants to broken climbing skins.

Of course the Nordic skier will also include a mini wax kit, with at least the next softest wax from whatever you start with, as well as a scraper and cork. If you expect to run into rapidly changing conditions on a long all-day tour, bring the whole selection—including some paraffin, and maybe a small butane torch if you anticipate putting on and removing klister on the trail (a real bother). Even Alpine skiers might carry a can of Toko 'touring' wax (white) to back up their skins; it weighs almost nothing. And, of course, appropriate downhill wax for the descent.

To turn your repair kit into a full emergency kit, add the minimum first aid material you think desirable (see chapter 8 for details) and the following: a water-tight container of matches, preferably waterproof as well; a large candle for starting a fire; and a very small waterproof tarp for emergency overnight protection, should the one-day tour stretch on beyond one day . . . a polyurethane sheet will do; a tiny 'space blanket' weighs less and is more compact. In Europe, tent-like bivouac sacks are very popular and enable one to survive the worst Alpine conditions. These might be a good idea for a high peak-bagging tour in the Rockies or the West.

Very few good skiers, touring for a few hours just to get a single run in steep untracked powder, ever think of carrying, much less using, an avalanche cord (see chapter 7). But they all should. An avalanche cord weighs hardly anything and it could save your life.

A map showing the route of your tour, and a compass if necessary, just about complete our list of extra items. The secret is not to take everything, just everything you'll need. And it's never the same twice.

A pocket knife is always in demand, especially by those who don't have one, if only for slicing salami and cheese for lunch. In the Alps, a corkscrew is essential. For some skiers, a corkscrew is essential anywhere.

Planning the tour

Diversity is the key to the one-day ski tour. The only sameness is in the use of skis and the absence of crowds. Without exhausting this variety, we can name several distinct types of one-day tours: the all-downhill tour, touring to a peak, the pure cross-country tour, and moonlight touring. A few examples, all drawn from the Sierra Nevada, the range the authors know best, will illustrate the unique flavor of each type of tour.

The *all-downhill tour*—is it really possible? This usually involves riding a ski lift to the highest point of a ski area, and then taking off in the opposite direction from the packed runs. It's an ideal way for the Alpine tourer to practice deep snow techniques. The destination of the tour is usually a road lower down, or another valley, village or ski area. The Squaw Peak-Alpine Meadows traverse in the Tahoe Sierra is such a tour. From the top of Squaw Valley's 'Siberia' chair lift, one climbs 500 feet to the summit of Squaw Peak. And then it's downhill all the way, in a beautiful hanging valley, hidden from the ski areas on either hand. Steep slopes (30 to 35 degrees) lead to the vast open slopes of the Sun Bowl. Then, entering a sparse forest, one skis down gentle slopes to the Five Lakes Basin, where frozen lakes make a spectacular picnic site. Afterwards, crossing a low ridge, a series of easy couloirs and open slopes takes you down to the Alpine Meadows road—hours of skiing in a grandiose setting, untracked snow and no people, next door to one of the biggest, most crowded resorts in the West. This type of tour can be found almost anywhere with a little imagination.

Touring to a peak is more in the tradition of Alpine touring, especially if steep slopes are involved, and the point of the tour is generally the view, and the run down. A beautiful example is the tour to Matterhorn Peak, up Horse Creek from Twin Lakes on the east side of the Sierra. On this high-altitude tour, one gains 3,000 feet in seven miles, following a series of interlocking valleys, to a shoulder just below the final rock slopes of Matterhorn Peak. Spring conditions are usually so good here that a four hour ascent is very reasonable. One often has to wait a few additional hours for the snow to soften to a perfect corn texture (the more ambitious scramble to the summit, others lie in the sun), and the run down is guaranteed to be one of the high points of any season. You lose track of the number of turns you've made; at the bottom you're exhausted but deliriously happy, drunk with skiing.

Pure cross-country touring. These are generally loop

tours or point-to-point tours, rather than climbing up only to ski down in your own tracks. Rolling terrain is better than precipitous slopes; and sprawling low ridges, gentle valleys and frozen lakes are ideal. A popular cross-country tour, on the gentle west slope of the Sierra, goes from Bear Valley on Hwy. 4 to Duck Lake some four miles away. The skier has his choice of several routes through open timbered slopes, so each trip, coming or going, is a new experience. The terrain is so gentle that one can make the whole tour without even knowing how to turn. (In the West one seldom finds completely flat country for cross-country skiing.)

Moonlight touring is not really a genre, but it is quite an experience. The combination of full moon and fresh powder may only occur once a season, but the touring skier who passes it up is crazy. You don't have to go anywhere, make any turns, or accomplish anything. Just being there on your skis in the liquid white silence is enough. This is where wilderness skiing blends into poetry.

To realize these and other kinds of short tours, a few basic principles of planning and organizing can help.

THE PARTY: Common sense should warn you not to tour alone. Three is the minimum safe party and four is much better. If someone is injured, one skier can stay with him, if need be, while the other two go for hlep. We've all broken this rule and gotten away with it, but what if. . . .

With whom do you tour? It's a good idea for beginners to take advantage of guided tours, and organized tours under the auspices of clubs or Nordic-oriented ski schools (which are still quite rare). You can learn just as much, and probably have a better time with a few experienced friends.

Touring with a party of other beginners is not too wise, but still better than not going at all. In this last case, where everyone is inexperienced, it's better to underestimate your skiing ability at first, especially in deciding how far to go.

Ideally the members of the party should know each other, and each other's skiing ability. This is not as critical on a day tour as on a long trip; you'll discover soon enough whether your friends are cheerful companions as well as good skiers. Besides you only have to be with them for a day, not a week, or a month. But that one day can be ruined if you lead someone into a skiing situation that's too difficult for him to handle.

Speaking of leading someone somewhere, we might mention that most ski tours don't need leaders (in the formal sense). It seems almost an American tradition in mountaineering to dispense with formal leadership. It is a good tradition. The wilderness skier is escaping from rules and formal structures in modern life. Why create new ones in the back country? Generally, decision-making is a collective process. The more critical the problem, the more you follow the experienced members of the group. If there's a real expert in the group—a skilled climber on steep dangerous terrain, or a doctor in case of injury—his leadership is taken for granted and emerges spontaneously, not by his being named 'leader.'

We are not advocating helter-skelter touring, with each skier going off on his own. To make this unstructured philosophy work, a general sense of responsibility must prevail. The group must stick together, both on the trail and mentally. Of course, the stronger members are more-or-less responsible for the weaker ones, but really everyone is (or should be) responsible for everyone else.

If you're on a guided tour, or out with an instructor, this doesn't really apply. The guide *is* the leader, it's *his* mountain or country, he knows it intimately and has something special to contribute. Even the most experienced wilderness skiers can learn something from a guide in an unfamiliar area. But with experience one tends to gather a circle of ski touring friends, and thus one's trips are mostly self-organized, rather than through clubs, schools and guide services.

THE ROUTE: How do you select a good tour? Usually on the basis of a friend's recommendation, often one of your party who wants to take his friends back to a spot that he has particularly enjoyed. There are a number of excellent guide books in print, describing touring possibilities in a whole region (see chapter 9). And you can obtain valuable route suggestions from any of the few touring ski schools or instructors in the country. But generally you just have a vague idea: wouldn't it be nice to go there? And you shouldn't be stopped by the fact that a given route hasn't been skied before, as far as you know.

The most useful tools for planning your route are the topographic map and, in the case of Alpine terrain at or above timberline, photographs. When available, photographs are more useful than maps since they give a better indication of the type of skiing you will encounter. On a one-day tour, the route by which you can ascend a peak is usually limited to the side closest to the road.

Two things to consider in picking your route are objective dangers and the means you will use to navigate the route. Some ski trails, particularly forested trails in the East, are marked with blazes. At other times map and compass will be your only guide (see chapter 6). But in general it's far easier to familiarize yourself with major terrain features and use them to steer by and keep the map as a reserve reference. Thus, it's often easier to tour along a gentle ridge line with a good view than in a densely wooded valley where you can't 'see the forest for the trees.' Objective dangers are those built-in to the environment (not arising from the skier's own actions) such as storms, falling rock on a mountain face, and most important for the skier, avalanches. Avalanches are covered in detail in chapter 7, but remember they are not a literary fiction or a theoretical danger. Every year a respectable number of back-country skiers get 'chopped' in avalanches as a result of ignoring basic rules. Generally, the Alpine skier is much more exposed to objective danger than the Nordic skier because of the steeper terrain he seeks out. Most of the danger potential of a ski tour can be assessed and eliminated by a little forethought at the planning stage.

Planning your route for maximum skiing pleasure also involves a little craftiness. Wherever possible we suggest loop-type trips, where you don't go out and come back in the same tracks. This variety makes the tour more interesting, but demands greater route-finding skills.

A valuable hint for planning spring ski tours is to follow the sun. By beginning the tour on southeast-facing slopes, hitting the north slopes around noon when the sun is highest, and finishing the tour in the evening on west facing slopes, you can often manage to ski on perfect snow all day long. Ideal spring snow, of course, is neither icy nor mushy, but rather hard with a couple of inches of soft sun-warmed surface—perfect corn. Terrain may make it impossible to 'follow the sun' but you can usually be in the right place at the right time at least once during the touring day. With this in mind, check the exposure or direction of the slopes as you study a map of the tour the night before.

ARE YOU READY? As you finish planning any tour, there are a few last points to check.

Is your equipment ready? Even the most experienced wilderness skier will forget key items simply because he put off assembling his gear to the last minute. Once you've been touring for a while, you'll have your own collection of stories about driving 100 miles to the mountains with a friend (never you) who forgot his *ski boots*. A good idea is to make up your own basic equipment list, and check it prior to departure. The challenge is to take the minimum, yet take enough.

Most touring skiers are in excellent physical shape, often in better shape than their equipment. Learn to be a bit fanatical in caring for your gear. On a tour you can't ski down to the nearest patrolman and ask him to fix your binding. Check it all out before you leave and make sure everything will last the tour: straps, bindings, skins, the baskets of your poles, etc.

Do you have a contingency plan? Ask yourself: what will we do if someone gets hurt, can we go for help, whom do we contact? What if there's a sudden storm, or a white-out? For that matter, have you remembered to check a weather report? Under what circumstances would you abandon the tour and turn back? Good touring practice does not lead to accidents, but the element of risk can never be reduced to zero. Thinking about these things beforehand will make an actual emergency, should it arise, much easier to deal with.

And finally, notify someone of your proposed tour:

route, estimated time, and the people involved. Even leaving a note on your car is better than nothing. National forest and park rangers and wardens are the logical people to notify if you're skiing in their areas. If you're touring near a major ski area, it might be wise to notify the ski patrol.

On the trail

'On the trail' is a loose expression. What we hope to cover in this section is the skiing strategy of a one-day tour—hints about applying your ski technique to the problems of moving over unfamiliar ground.

GETTING UNDERWAY: Whatever your plans for the day, an early start will help realize them. In late spring your efficiency drops by half, once you are in the full blast of the sun. Of course there's nothing wrong with an eleven o'clock start or an afternoon tour, if your route is short and the snow is not too soft.

Once underway, there's a certain period of adjustment to the exhilaration of being so far from the city and to the problems at hand. Suppose it's a late winter tour after a recent snowfall, a two-day thaw and a sudden cold snap. The snow will have a rock-hard crust so you start out carrying your skis, only to find that in open meadows the snow has softened. On with the skis. Then a jar or can or perhaps the brandy flask (not on the equipment list) is digging viciously into your back; so you stop to adjust your load and pad the offending object with a sweater. Moments later you're overheated, so you stop again to remove parka, jacket, or even gaiters. But not twenty minutes later, a wind springs up and you put them all back on. The snow gets softer and wetter, and begins to freeze on the bottom of your skis which must be scraped.

In short, it's often hard to get going, to find your pace in the morning. But it's a great game, and the skier who is crafty can avoid half the stops and hassles with a little thought. On cold crisp mornings people have a lot of energy which is usually wasted by rushing off too fast, and becoming overtired or overheated in the first miles, or the first few hundred yards. Unless the start is a downhill run, you won't need to bother with any warming or stretching exercises; a few minutes walking does very well.

ON THE LEVEL AND UPHILL: Finding the right *pace*, then, is crucial. The right pace for your condition, the terrain and your style of skiing. Nordic skiers will be moving quite rapidly after a few minutes. Alpine skiers tend to plod like patient donkeys, their minds fixed on the run to come, or simply thinking of other things.

On steep uphills, where even the Nordic skier slows to a snail's pace, the *rest step* is invaluable. This slow walk, with a pause between each step, has been described in virtually all mountaineering texts, but without what we consider its most essential feature: the coordination of breathing with the step. Breathing-out demands muscular effort, breathing in is a phase of relative relaxation. The strong expulsion of air should come at the same time as the bent front leg is straightening to lift the body's weight up the slope. The other foot is then slid forward, and the skier pauses an instant with no weight on this new front foot. This rest phase is synchronized with the inhalation of a new breath, a relaxed expansion of chest and diaphragm as air rushes in to fill the void left by a strong out-breath.

Farfetched? Not at all. It works. The idea of concentrating on breathing-out is very much a part of different yoga systems, and is the secret of the prodigious physical efforts of aging Japanese zen masters. The out-breath is synchronized with the moment of strongest muscular effort; then the whole body—lungs and muscles—relaxes for an instant before the next expiration/effort. This type of rest step will double your stamina on steep uphill grinds, but it takes a little concentration at first. Should your breathing get out of phase with the lifting effort of your legs, you will rapidly get out of breath.

If the slope is too steep for any ski climbing techniques, put the skis on your pack, and climb directly up on foot, using your poles as canes.

Keeping an even steady pace can be quite difficult in very deep and heavy, or lightly crusted snow. It's fatiguing to break trail, and frustratingly slow to follow behind. The best advice is not to be a hero, and rotate the lead frequently. Sliding your ski straight forward in deep snow (over your knees) can result in a tendency for the ski tip to dive and bury itself deeper in the snow mass. Instead, shuffle your foot backwards and then lift the tip toward the surface on each step forward.

Stream Crossings present unorthodox hazards. (How embarrassing to drown on a ski tour.) Normally, streams can be crossed on snow bridges, after first examining these natural structures very carefully to determine their load-carrying possibilities (the thicker the better). By 'scissoring' one ski ahead of the other, and shuffling gently, you can spread your weight further and more evenly over the snow bridge. Bare logs, obviously, require removing one's skis, and may be slippery with ice and rime. It's conceivable that an experienced mountaineer could rig a 'tyrolean' or rope traverse across a wide and raging torrent, but such crossings are better avoided. Should someone fall in, the party must stop, dry him and warm him, dressing him as much as possible in the dry spare clothes of other members, and if necessary build a fire to do the job. A soaked skier is in a very serious position indeed.

DOWNHILL: As a general rule, the best skier should go first—both to test out the snow, and scout the most reasonable line of descent for the other members of the party. (Of course, this applies also to level and uphill skiing, whenever route-finding problems are involved.) The exception, however, is a descent in the sort of deep powder where a fallen skier can have trouble getting up, especially with a pack. This is not infrequent in the West, and anyone who has spent ten minutes floundering around upside down in the snow, trying to get back on his feet (even without a pack), will know just how serious this can be. In such cases a competent skier should go first, but the best powder skier should bring up the rear and help extricate any trapped bodies. A powder skier can become trapped, too, by skiing into one of the deep hollows or 'moats' that form around large trees. Steer well clear. We know of several cases where a solitary powder skier (rule No. 1: don't ski alone.) was trapped upside down in one of the moats, hanging from his wedged skis for hours, and one case where the skier died.

The main question on the descent, however, is: How hard should one ski? The classical answer, generally delivered with an air of grey-bearded wilderness wisdom, has been to take it easy, to ski with extreme prudence as soon as one leaves the practice area, and always to sacrifice a beautiful, dynamic, flowing descent for a slow, timid, controlled one. We are not against control, or prudence, or the time-honored stem christie; but we disagree, in part, with this advice.

It is our experience that skiers who are overly nervous about the descent and trying consciously to make gentle, hesitant turns with a large margin for 'chickening out,' *are the skiers most likely to be injured.* Any fear of the snow, any holding back, leads to a loss of balancing reflexes and a muscular contraction that can transform a gentle fall into a sprain, strain, or broken leg. In skiing the back-country, just as on the packed slope, fear is the greatest problem, and the greatest contributor to injury. So we would say: *If you think you can ski a slope with a given turn or technique, then ski it as aggressively as possible.* This doesn't mean doing 'jet' christies down every slope with a big pack. Rather, figure out first if you can ski it, then how you're going to ski it, and finally *attack.* This feeling of attack is absolutely necessary if you are going to master difficult snow: wind drifts, sastrugi, crust and slop.

Judgment is the crux. If it's obvious you can't really handle the downhill run, remember you can always get down anything with linked traverses and kick turns. This is a much better alternative than making out-of-control snow-plows and frightened stem christies.

The above advice is really meant for Alpine-style skiers. Nordic skiers, more conscious of the limitations of their technique and equipment, are generally already enjoying a long, graceful and secure traverse down the hill, while their Alpine brethren are still asking themselves if they can ski it. And this leads to our last topic.

SAFETY: Clearly, safe touring is more the result of judgment than of following a set of rules, and judgment comes only from experience. While you're out gaining that experience, here are a few points to keep in mind.

Don't split your party. If one or two members of your group are separated, they don't really need to be lost to create confusion and panic, or ruin your tour. Neither group knows what the other is doing, whether they're lost, whether they need help. The more fit members of the party simply have to restrain their enthusiasm to rush ahead, leaving the rest to straggle along in their tracks. Offering to carry part of a slower skier's load might even things up. Likewise, the stronger members should watch for signs of fatigue or exhaustion in the slower ones. If whoever is leading sets a good pace, there won't be any exhaustion or undue fatigue.

Confusion is certainly the least serious consequence of splitting the party. Two friends of ours were climbing a Sierra peak on skis, when a rising wind and freezing temperature led them to draw up their parka hoods tightly over their eyes, and in the following gusts they lost sight of each other. One of them waited for his companion at the base of the summit cone for over an hour in appalling conditions, while his friend was relaxing in the luxury of a small shack on the summit that housed some television relay equipment.

Don't daydream—at least not too much. It is all too easy to lose yourself in the beauty of the surroundings, the rhythm of your movements, the simple exhilaration of wilderness skiing, and forget more critical things like the time and the weather. Keep alert for cloud build-up and sudden wind shifts, or dense fog-like cloud banks creeping up from lower valleys to enshroud you in a possible afternoon whiteout. Likewise you should know if you are making good time, or if your party is unusually slow, too slow perhaps to complete the tour before nightfall. Both these factors can seriously modify your plans and affect the success of the tour. Be aware of them early.

At the same time, keep an eye on major terrain features and landmarks, (try to remember if you've crossed two creeks or three, etc.). This awareness of the terrain could be precious if fog or storm sets in. As we've indicated, a map and compass are all right in theory, but it's better not to be forced to rely on them exclusively.

Be willing to turn back. All the above factors can in some degree render difficult, unlikely, or highly dangerous, the successful completion of your proposed ski tour. Remember there are no rules, and no prizes are awarded for climbing a given peak, or completing a given route. Knowing why and when to turn back, or call short a beautiful tour, is the toughest test of a wilderness skier's judgment. Actually, turning back can seem to be a tougher decision than pressing foolishly on, in the face of darkening clouds, rising wind and the first snow flurries. There are no absolutes here; it's possible to have a great tour in a snowstorm. But if you're touring with skiers weaker than yourself, always err on the side of prudence in making such decisions.

Safe ski touring means recognizing and respecting real dangers in the winter landscape. Subjective danger is avoided by knowing one's limits of stamina and experience, and the limits of one's ski technique. The principal objective dangers are bad weather and avalanches. Hostile weather, although it can overtake you suddenly in a matter of hours, is still direct, brutal and obvious. Avalanches, on the other hand, are subtle and mysterious things. After seasons of avalanche control work, forest service experts still confess to uneasy hunches about certain slopes, still admit how little they know about avalanches, and never lose their respect for the power and danger of even the smallest avalanche.

Avalanches are the major hazard in wilderness skiing, so you should learn as much about them as possible. Read chapter 7 on snow and avalanches, but remember that it's only an introduction and summary of a big subject. Since new snowfalls provide the most exciting skiing *and* the highest avalanche danger, we can only repeat our general warning. Be aware of the danger, learn what you can about it, and ski with great caution in areas of high avalanche risk.

It seems unfair to end a chapter on the pleasures and techniques of the short, one-day ski tour with a grim warning. Fortunately, the dangerous situations we encounter while touring are few. The beauties, the satisfactions of ski touring are, by contrast, almost infinite. If we devote a lot of pages to mere technique, it's because this is, after all, a handbook for the wilderness skier. The esthetic and emotional side of mountain and touring skiing, fortunately, doesn't need to be explained in words.

In the next chapter we shall see how to extend our skills to winter camping, cooking and survival, so that ultimately we may continue skiing, day after day, through untracked country.

5. Multi-Day Ski Tours

Surely the ultimate in wilderness skiing is to take off, not for a few hours, but for days on end—letting your skis carry you further and further from the city scene, deeper and deeper into a secret white world. Returning from a short one-day tour one often wonders why it had to end. It doesn't. In this chapter we will cover the techniques and equipment needed for staying out day after day, camping comfortably in the middle of winter. But first a word about the various styles of multi-day ski touring.

In Europe, both in Scandinavia and in the Alps, many more people go on long, multi-day ski tours than in this country. This is due to the enormous number of overnight huts, which greatly simplify the problems of a long tour. In Europe, you can leave the tent at home, and often food and fuel as well, so that it's no more complicated to tour for a week than for a day. Unfortunately, there are relatively few ski-touring huts in this country, although there will be more in the future. (It's becoming clear that huts can actually reduce the impact of uncontrolled and often destructive camping in summer). If there is any good hut-touring in your area we heartily recommend it; either skiing from hut to hut, or skiing to a hut from which you can climb and descend the surrounding slopes and peaks. Since you will be lightly laden, hut-touring combines all the pleasures of high-powered skiing, with the ineffable sensation of remoteness and detachment that comes with prolonged periods spent away from the nearest car or road.

When huts are not available, the long tour takes on a different flavor. Everything slows down. Since snow-camping in winter demands more and better equipment than camping in summer, packs are almost always large and heavy. Even the experienced Nordic skier has to slow his pace, and downhill skiing likewise becomes more restrained, less aggressive. The final result is more an *exploration-oriented* adventure than a *sport-oriented* adventure, as the one-day tour often is. But despite the extra chores and heavier packs, you will experience an unusual sense of freedom on multi-day tours. For most mountain lovers, backpackers or climbers, winter snow is like a 'Do Not Enter' sign hung up on their favorite hills—and here you are, traveling at will and enjoying it. You can go anywhere. You can stay as long as you want. You have become a complete wilderness skier.

Not yet, though. To get there we must cover two major topics, *shelter* and *food*. The actual skiing on a long tour varies only in degree and length from what we've covered so far; so, aside from suggesting a few equipment modifications for long tours, we will say no more about skiing. Finally, the chapter will close with a few tips on organizing a long ski tour and the psychological aspects of keeping the party functioning harmoniously in the back country.

Overnight Shelter

To the wilderness skier, shelter means more than just a roof over one's head. The problem is twofold: shelter from the harsher elements like driving wind and falling snow; and insulation, not just from cold but from the conductive properties of cold, damp snow. Adequate shelter is everything that guarantees you a warm, comfortable night out, starting with your sleeping bag.

SLEEPING GEAR: Good down-filled sleeping bags are

more readily available today than they were when most of us began touring—and nearly twice as expensive. Everything considered, however, superior design, workmanship and top materials make it cheaper in the long run to buy the best bags available. We've already suggested several low-cost alternatives in assembling your ski equipment, but there's not much you can do about sleeping bags. It is difficult to find a quality bag anywhere for under $75, but on the other hand, such a bag should last for years.

Your sleeping bag should be of lightweight nylon (1.9 oz. is common). Very few bags have overlapping-tube construction, nor is it necessary; but slanted wall baffles between the down compartments seem to be better than straight ones. The baffling material ideally should be a light, 'elastic' nylon mesh, less prone to ripping out. The bag should be differentially cut (the inside diameter smaller than the outside) to avoid undue wrinkling and pressing of the layers together to form cold spots. Theoretically, a cocoon-shaped 'mummy' or contoured bag without a zipper is the most efficient in terms of warmth versus weight. But addition of a full-length zipper gives you the versatility of a summer bag as well. Sure signs of poor design are metal zippers, narrow gauge small-toothed plastic zippers, or zippers in the center rather than down the side of the bag. But a list of good qualities (as well as these few warnings) is fortunately almost superfluous, since most well-known manufacturers make only first quality bags.

The real question in choosing a winter bag is: Which model, and how much down filling, do I need? Our advice may sound odd for the rigors of winter camping, but we feel that the most practical bags for ski touring are the lightest models. Like any piece of equipment a sleeping bag can be overdesigned, and most have been. The average

catalogue selection shows at least three main types. The
so-called "lightweight" model, a very contoured bag which,
by implication, is only for summer, and even then only for
spartan types. A 'comfort' model, cut wider and roomier,
but with the same basic construction. And a so-called
'winter' or 'expedition' model, an enormously thick bag
with complex baffling systems, pounds and pounds of
down, and an astronomic number of inches of loft. This last
model is generally referred to in catalogue prose as the
'ultimate' bag; but unless you go above 20,000 feet, you
will probably never even get to zip it up all the way. The
lightweight bag, on the other hand, is often the best designed bag of the line. It is cut very narrow on the inside, so
there is less space to be filled in its down tubes. And thus,
less down can actually keep you warmer in many cases.

We have used this type of bag in some pretty cold places
(Alaska and Patagonia) with great luck. A few times we've
been obliged to wear our down jackets for extra warmth.
Yet this is a practical solution for extreme cases, since the
down jacket is sure to be in your kit anyway. (Our tentative
conclusion is that most catalogues make the bigger, roomier
sleeping bags sound more attractive simply because they
cost more—a parallel to automobile advertising.)

One last point. Overstuffing a bag with down won't
make it any warmer. For a given size of down tube, there is
an optimum fill that will expand this tube to its maximum
dimensions; more down is just added weight. On the other
hand, the down tubes may be slightly under-filled, and you
won't know it for a couple of months until the bag seems
to 'go flat'. If you have experienced friends, find out what
kind of bags they use when touring, and look at an old bag
to see how it's stood up to use before buying a new one.

Sleeping pads are an absolute necessity in winter, not a luxury. The air mattress is dead; convection currents within the tubes actually cool you off, instead of insulating you from the snow. Foam or ensolite pads are lighter, cheaper and more efficient. Thick foam pads are indisputably more comfortable. But their greater bulk generally rules out a full-length pad, and then you must deal with the problem of touching the cold tent floor with your legs, feet, or heels.

Thin closed-cell foam, like ensolite, seems perfect. Even thin ensolite pads don't feel as hard as in summer, since the snow is somewhat plastic and will 'give' and 'form' beneath you. A 3/8" ensolite pad is standard for winter camping, but many people find that 1/4" pads are sufficient. They are much lighter and less bulky. So much so, in fact, that on several trips we have carried two 1/4" ensolite pads per person, and then combined them, like Japanese tatami mats, to form a complete, solid floor across a four-man tent or an ice cave.

No one needs instructions on how to fall asleep—but here's a tip for keeping your boots from freezing if they've gotten wet during the day. Take the stuff sack of your sleeping bag, turn it inside out (so the bag won't get dirty later), put your boots inside, and place the whole thing beneath your sleeping bag—just under the knees. This is a comfortable position and your boots should be warm if not dry in the morning. You can also dry wet gloves, socks, etc. inside your sleeping bag.

LARGER PACKS: To carry your sleeping bag, foam pad, *and* your fair share of everything else (such community items as tentage, stove, fuel, food and so forth), you will need a larger pack than for day touring. There are several options: a bigger-sized, classical frameless rucksack, a specifically designed frameless pack, or the traditional pack-frame and bag.

Serious touring skiers often prefer large-size European-style rucksacks (Millet from France, Salewa from Germany, Karrimore from England) for their high capacity and inherent stability when used with a waist strap. Their narrow cut, originally developed for climbing, also keeps the pack from protruding too far to the rear. The classic Norwegian Bergans-type rucksack has fallen into disfavor because, although large enough, its pear-like shape bulks out too far when fully loaded, forcing the skier to tilt forward to preserve balance.

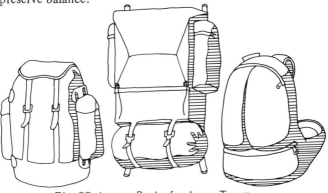

Fig. 23. Larger Packs for Long Tours

Contoured aluminum packframes and bags are standard for heavy packing, summer and winter, but create problems for the wilderness skier. They are effective precisely because they carry the load close to the back and *high* over the shoulders. But this last feature makes them very tippy, with a lot of lateral sway (these packs are designed for slow walking, not running). And this tippiness constantly threatens the skier's balance on the descent. On long ski treks of several weeks there is, unfortunately, almost no other choice. On the descent, you must loosen the shoulder straps to lower the pack's center of gravity, cinch-up the waist band, and do your best. Use your poles more than normally for balance, and avoid brusque up-unweighting movements. It's also possible to move the packbag to the lower part of the frame, putting sleeping bag and foam pad on top instead of underneath; this will help lower the center of gravity and stabilize the pack somewhat. If you must ski with a packframe, choose a directly attached shoulder strap, not the 'free-floating' yoke style which has more sway.

Another compromise solution is to combine a large nylon rucksack with a child's-size aluminum packframe. This is a lot less tippy than a full-size, high, contoured packframe for skiing downhill. And while not nearly as comfortable for walking, it is still far better than a plain rucksack for the heavy loads that are standard on a major ski-mountaineering effort.

The wilderness skier's dream is a rucksack, low and stable, that functions like a packframe, high and slender. The closest we have seen is the amazing Don Jensen-designed frameless pack: a strange-looking, compartmentalized, wrap-around, contoured rucksack, long and wide—yet thin enough to cling to the skier's back (see fig. 23). It is large enough for trips as long as a week, and after that there are no perfect solutions. The Jensen design is not the only attempt at modifying a basic rucksack (with compartments or semi-frames) to improve its performance; nor will it be the last. But so far we think it is the most successful.

All skiing packs should be waterproof (except perhaps against the back to minimize sweating) because they will spend a lot of time on the snow—either as lunchtime seats or burdens thrown aside in sheer frustration at a rest stop. No overnight pack—even with the lightest, featherweight bag, the thinnest ensolite pad, and all the rest to match—is ever light enough.

On some tours, over easy rolling country, it is possible to eliminate packs altogether by using a special skier's sled designed for long Nordic tours. The sled is attached to the skier's waist by two fiberglass wands which don't interfere with his diagonal stride. These light Scandinavian sleds are virtually unknown in this country, imported in small numbers and very hard to find. But for certain tours, this could be the best solution for carrying overnight gear—or children too young to ski.

TENTS: We have already hinted that the ideal ski shelter is a cabin, complete with fireplace or at least a guitar hanging on the wall, and also mentioned how few such huts exist in America. The common substitute, with more wilderness flavor anyhow, is the two or four-man mountain tent. But they are not cheap (and it's difficult to make a satisfactory one yourself). Unlike the quality sleeping bags, almost any one of which is suitable for winter camping, not all so--called 'mountain' tents are really suitable for snow camp-ing. In choosing a good ski tent, look for the following:

Light weight. Your tent should weigh not more than 3 lbs. per person, so that a two-man tent should weigh no more than 6 lbs., and a four-man tent from 10 to 12 lbs.

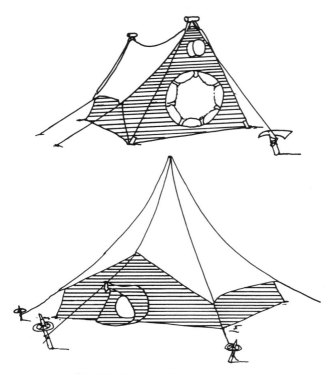

Fig. 24. Typical Mountain Tents

Functional Design. A ski-touring tent should be large enough for you to bring packs and gear inside; and should be designed to spill the wind. The best tents have a so-called 'catenary cut', (the panel and ridge lines are cut on a curve to draw tight without wrinkling). Poles should be of light sectional aluminum that fasten top *and bottom* to the tent (otherwise they will sink into the snow). Waterproof fabric on the floor and a few inches up the side is essential. A cooking hole, covered by a zippered flap, in the door is very handy. Two-man tents are usually around 4-1/2' by 7' and almost 4 feet high. For four men, a pyramid shape, roughly 7 or 8 feet square, with three or four external poles, is typical. External poles save so much room that on one ski trip we slept six men comfortably in a four-man tent. Tents should have a tunnel/sleeve door and good ventilators; a second zippered door is a fine idea.

Fabric. Modern tents are made from light nylon, usually with a rip-stop weave, weighing under 2 oz. per sq. yd. Such fabric is windproof, yet allows some air transfer or 'breathing.' Lower walls and floor are of the same material (or slightly heavier), waterproofed with a polythene coating.

These tents are sold with waterproof 'fly sheets' which can be left home in winter unless you're expecting rain. Even so, condensation is always a problem in cold weather. Sleeping bags are invariably damp in the morning, but will dry rapidly if suspended in the sun from skis while you are organizing things around camp. Small vertical side walls on the tent are a great help in keeping bags and everything else dry. The less you touch the tent the drier you'll be, even in a well-ventilated, permeable tent. Finally, some tents can be equipped with 'frost liners' of light mesh cloth to trap condensing frost and keep it from falling on your bags. The idea is great, but most people who try them eventually throw them away in sheer frustration, as they complicate the already complicated problem of tent living.

Choosing your campsite is seldom the problem that

mountaineering handbooks make out, because you often
don't have much choice. Try for a sheltered location, easy
access to water (if there is any) and a good view. Although
it should be obvious, remember not to camp beneath possible avalanche paths or slopes. Use trees as a windbreak, but
avoid pitching the tent directly beneath them, as snow
falling from high branches could collapse your tent. A
valley bottom is usually a colder tent site than a bench a
hundred feet up.

Pitching the tent is fast work if you stay organized and
everyone helps. Keep your skis on to pack the tent platform, then boot-pack it even harder. Spread the tent floor
out on the snow with the door (or zippered door) away
from the wind. You can use skis and poles very effectively
to anchor corners and guy lines. Small aluminum disks
make very good anchors for holding the main load-bearing
lines. Some tents have snow flaps on which snow is piled to
keep wind from blowing under the tent.

Severe conditions are more often encountered when
camping above timberline than in the forest. These might
be lack of flat ground to pitch the tent, heavy winds, or a
heavy new snowfall (which can happen anywhere). A tent
platform can be cut with one's skis, but it's better to carry
a light aluminum snow shovel which has a dozen other uses.
The snow shovel will also permit you to cut snow blocks to
form a windbreak wall on one side of an exposed tent—a lot
less work than digging a cave, but often sufficient to get a
peaceful night's sleep in the middle of a windstorm. Insert-
ing a large rubber band or shock cord into the guy lines
(before the trip, of course) helps minimize the flapping of
the tent in high winds, by absorbing the shock of sudden
gusts.

A heavy new snowfall is always cause for concern. It can bury a tent completely, cutting off ventilation to the interior, and suffocation becomes a real possibility unless something is done quickly. In a major blizzard, you will probably have to dig out your tent periodically, and perhaps even re-pitch it on the new higher surface. If the storm is a long-one, you might be better off digging a snow cave.

SNOW CAVES AND IGLOOS: These are by far the finest, warmest, most secure shelters for winter or high-mountain camping. The rub is that they are never available, but must be dug at the price of considerable effort. Still, it's often worth it.

Since it invariably takes several hours to dig a good snow cave, it is not too practical to rely on constructing one every evening of a long, on-going trip. Tents, after all, can be put up in a few moments with every little effort. But if severe storms should pin you down for a few days, or if you plan to use one camp as a base for several days skiing, then a snow cave is ideal.

To dig your cave you must find a slope of consolidated snow; the vertical wall of a small wind drift is perfect. (On flat glaciers you will have to build an igloo.) Next, at least two diggers: one to attack the snow with short, stabbing shovel strokes, and one to shovel the debris back out of the entrance as the cave is enlarged. Put on parkas and overpants first (or anything waterproof) as it is a wet job—especially at first, when you must dig a narrow entrance tunnel on your knees. And of course, shovels. The light aluminum snow shovel already mentioned is adequate only in the best of conditions; use it solely for clearing debris, as a hard snow surface will crumple it. For serious snow-cave excavat-

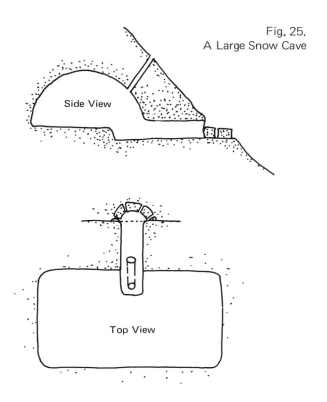

Fig. 25.
A Large Snow Cave

Side View

Top View

ing (if you're really counting on being able to do it) take a small shovel with a pointed steel blade. A 'D' handle is convenient, not essential.

The basic snow cave is a small entrance tunnel which expands after a few feet into a dome-shaped room. The roof need not be high enough for you to stand up, but a completely rounded wall/roof profile is very important in strengthening the cave. The first night you spend in a snow cave, you will probably worry about it collapsing; everyone does. If the walls and roof are rounded into a continuous arch, you will sleep a lot easier, and the cave, which always sags after a while, will last a lot longer without repairs.

A snow cave for four or more people begins to exhibit certain design refinements. A classic design is to extend two sleeping 'wings' on either side of a central area used for cooking and eating. (See fig. 25) It's a good idea to have the sleeping area higher than the entrance. But don't turn the entrance into a complicated maze, at least not until you've finished scooping all the loose snow out of the cave.

Once the cave is dug, poke ventilation holes through to the outside, and protect the door from drifting shut with snow. (A small square of visqueen makes a good flap entrance, and a protective wall of snow blocks can screen the entrance from wind.) Then lay down some sort of waterproof groundsheet, construct a floor of ensolite pads if you have enough, and move in.

Snow cave living can be a real treat. The temperature is cool, hovering around freezing, but never really cold. And a small candle or a stove at dinner time warms things up surprisingly. Small alcoves can be cut in the walls to store odds and ends, and the cave soon feels like home. Out of prudence, keep the digging tools *inside* the cave in case you have to dig your way out after a heavy snow fall. (Snow has some porosity, so you are less likely to have trouble breathing in a buried cave, than in a buried tent.) The shovel is also useful for periodically scraping away the accumulation of soft wet snow that forms small rounded stalactites on the roof wherever shovel blows have left small ridges. (Otherwise you'll have a drippy cave after a few days.) This half-melted soggy snow is ideal for making water, and more snow for melting can be chipped out of a specially reserved 'clean' corner of the cave.

When leaving your snow cave for the day, make sure it is obviously marked so that you can find it easily on your return. A drifted-over cave looks just like any other drift. Once on Mt. Fitz Roy in Patagonia, we temporarily lost Camp II in this way, and with it half of our equipment. We spent a few hours anxiously probing a wide snowslope until one of us accidentally fell into the cave.

On flat snowy plains and glaciers, the igloo replaces the snow cave—but only when the temperature is freezing or below. It is more work to build, and a small folding saw is a useful addition to the shovel in cutting and trimming snow blocks. There are dozens of variations on the basic plan which is familiar to every schoolboy—after your first attempt at building one, you will become an instant expert. A few hints. Build the smallest practical size, for strength as well as ease of construction. One builder stands inside the wall, one outside. To enlarge an igloo, dig the floor down another foot or so.

Improving the basic igloo is a great pastime on stormy days. We have seen split-level igloos, linked together by secondary tunnels and spiralling ramps. There is a little of *homo faber*, man the builder, in all of us.

BIVOUACS: A bivouac is a more-or-less unplanned, more-or-less improvised night out. In a sense, bivouacking is camping with minimum (or less than minimum) gear, a more reasonable activity in summer than winter. Alpinists often use nylon bivouac sacks or small bivouac tents. These, or the classic tube tent, might be useful as minimum overnight shelter on a spring ski tour, where severe conditions are not anticipated. A really practical ski bivouac tent, pitched only with skis and poles, has yet to be designed.

The unplanned bivouac, however, is a real test for the wilderness skier; his very survival depends on his ingenuity in making his own shelter. A small snow cave is best. But if you don't have the tools or a good location, use a snow trench bivouac.

Let's suppose you and a friend are skiing down out of the high peaks into the forest, and night overtakes you some miles from your cabin. It has been snowing for several hours and looks as though it will snow all night; all you have are small packs with a little extra lunch, down jackets and parkas. A fire is out of the question, since you've forgotten the matches. What now? Using your skis, dig a small trench, just large enough for you to sit in, completely below the surface. Line the bottom of the trench with broken-off tree branches. Place your skis and poles across the top of the trench, and then more boughs crisscrossing on top of them. Put on all your spare clothes, loosen your boots and put your feet in the pack (unless you need it to sit on), and settle down for an uncomfortable but bearable night. The roof, like the trees above, should collect the snow and keep you dry, and you will pass the night safely to ski away in the morning.

The basic idea in a bivouac is to get out of the wind (or snow), use all available insulation, and try to relax and rest as you wait for morning. Snow is the best insulation you'll find *as long as you're not sitting on it.* You will be warmer surrounded by snow than in the open air, especially in bad weather. There is a myth, current for centuries, about not going to sleep for fear of freezing. This is only true in cases of terminal exhaustion. If you can sleep in a bivouac, so much the better; you'll have more energy the next morning. Panic, fear, and anxiety can all contribute to decreasing your physical reserves and bringing you one step nearer to hypothermia or frostbite. (See chapter 8.)

Building a good fire is one of the best solutions for a forced bivouac. It's not as hard to build a fire in the snow as you might think, although it's harder to find resinous dead branches than in summer. If the wood is wet, you can scrape away the damp outside to get at the dry core, but generally a candle or chemical fire starter is necessary. Should fire building prove futile, dig a snow trench bivouac and get in it as soon as possible.

In the last analysis, solving the problem of shelter on a ski tour is more a question of judgment than of equipment. This is nowhere more true than in an emergency situation. Your best shelter will come from keeping your wits about you, and acting calmly and decisively. Survival equipment does not guarantee survival, but common sense generally does. A few hours practicing the construction of caves, igloos and emergency shelters might also help tip the scales.

Good eats

The major difference between camp cookery in summer and on a winter ski tour is that, generally, the snow camper must melt his water from snow. This changes everything to some degree. It is an additional chore, which prolongs the

time devoted to preparing meals, increases the fuel con-
sumption of the stoves, and adds to the general confusion
of an already crowded and cluttered tent. There are other
special problems, such as the necessity to use stoves, since
most burnable wood is buried beneath the snow. But by
and large, choosing and preparing food for a multi-day ski
tour is quite the same as preparing food for any summer
knapsacking or backpacking trip.

In this age of freeze-dried strawberry ice cream, turkey
tetrazzini and naturally grown, lecithin-impregnated Cha-
pati vegetable burgers, the wilderness skier pondering the
menu for his weekend tour may rightly experience a certain
confusion. He is faced with an ever-increasing proliferation
of dehydrated, freeze-dried and natural 'organic' foods,
both from specialized backpacking shops and in the supermarket. Frankly, we prefer shopping in the supermarket.
Many special backpackers' dehydrated menus are overdesigned, complicated to prepare in winter, and invariably
more expensive than the same items bought separately in
the market. When there was less to choose from (and dried
mashed potatoes were the standard), supermarket shopping
for a ski tour was a simple process, not a brain-fogging
march along rows of brightly-packaged nutrients.

Simplicity is the secret. We have one ski-touring friend
who can buy all the food for a 14 man-day ski tour in less
than thirty minutes at the local market, without a shopping
list. His secret is an aggressive selection of simple foods plus
a great variety of seasoning, a few—but only a few—delica-
cies and a gourmet's skill in preparation. The theme-and-
variations effect of a couple of basic menus is probably
better than trying to make each meal really different. It can
be the same almost every time, without tasting the same.

FOOD SELECTION: First a little theory. The food list may be broken into three basic elements: carbohydrates (starch and sugar), protein and fats. Carbohydrates are easiest to digest, proteins are next and fats are the most difficult. On the other hand, fats contain more than twice the caloric value of either protein or carbohydrates. (Butter has about 3250 calories per pound and olive oil has 4010.) On short, weekend trips, the balance of these nutritive elements is not crucial, and you can get away with some pretty lop-sided meals. The longer the trip, however, the more important it is to get enough of everything every day.

The following is a good framework for the selection of foods on a long trip. It was put to a severe but successful test by the expedition which climbed the long and difficult Hummingbird Ridge on Mt. Logan in the Yukon. The suggested weights are the *dry weight* of the food you take with you; adding water to reconstitute a dehydrated dish does *not* add any nutrients to what you've already got.

	Pounds per man-day
Starches	.9
Sugars	.4
Protein	.6
Fats & fatty foods	.25
Beverages (fruit powders, etc.)	.1
TOTAL	2.25 lbs./man-day

(A detailed list of foods in each category is found in appendix A.)

This 2 1/4 pounds per person per day will yield from 4300 to 4500 calories—adequate for almost all strenuous

winter ski tours, not to mention mountaineering expeditions. The total requirement for each category of food is
found by multiplying the above daily quantities by the
number of man-days you plan to be on the tour.

We confess to having bought food for some pretty long
trips without having consulted lists like the above. Once
you're experienced in such things, the end result is nearly
the same. You begin to think in terms of favorite menus,
which, if they have remained popular, probably represent
the desired proportions. At some point, though, the mind
boggles and you have to get out pencil and paper and start
planning your menus in greater detail.

Individual taste may lead to slight variations in the above
ratios. It's most important to take food you enjoy eating,
and that it be as light as possible (light packages and low
water content). On overnight tours, fresh foods are fine.
Whatever foods you select, take the time to package them
for the tour. Lost time and agony will be saved if loose
items like salt, sugar, powdered milk, etc., are packaged in
double plastic bags with tie loops or plastic clamps. Cans
and bottles should only be considered if there are strong
backs willing to carry them. Cooking oil may be taken in a
tightly capped plastic flask. Some people are very keen on
packaging a whole day's food together; but most of the
time this is too much bother, and definitely works against
creative cooking on the tour. The following are some meal
ideas that have worked well for us.

BREAKFAST: The simplest breakfast seems to be a hot
drink and some kind of cereal, either the instant or quick-
cooking variety, or the beloved 'crunchy granola.' Cold
cereals become warm ones when eaten with hot milk or

chocolate; and butter, sugar, raisins or other dried fruit can always be added to the pot. Anything more than this seems to us a real luxury breakfast: powdered egg mixes, tinned pre-cooked bacon, fried tortillas—all are possible but seldom worth it. Early morning skiing is often the best, so why waste it cooking brunch?

LUNCH: Lunch is always the same and, somehow, always good. Chocolate (or other sweets), meat (salami, landjaeger, liverwurst) or sardines, cheese (an infinite choice) and bread (dense pumpernickel in foil will last forever), have composed the classical mountain lunch since the days of Geoffery Winthrop Young and Sir Arnold Lunn. Hard candies and fruit drops are great on the trail; in fact, several snack-stops are probably more efficient and *sympathique* than one big lunch. On shorter trips, oranges and tangerines are much appreciated. We suggest a full water bottle (plastic) for each member of the party. Powdered fruit juice and fruit-flavored instant iced tea are often easier to drink than water.

DINNER: This is *the meal* of the day. Its preparation usually starts as soon as the tent is pitched or the party is installed in the snow cave, igloo, cabin or whatever. In cramped surroundings—one is rarely able to cook outside in winter—cooking the evening meal is a constant struggle to stay organized. If you have to melt snow for water, start as soon as possible, and fill up all available water bottles and containers before attacking the meal itself. Someone other than the cook should be willing to keep ducking outside with a pot to scrape up more snow for melting. This settling-down period is when most snow gets knocked into the tent, so be careful if you want to keep everything dry.

Even a large party of six will probably only have one stove going. So preparing the meal has to be an orderly, well-thought out procedure; needless to say, one-pot meals are almost a necessity. The classical ski-touring dinner seems to run somewhat like this: A cup of soup to start. Then the main stew-like dinner dish. It's good to use another batch of soup as a base for this dish instead of plain water. Into this goes a carbohydrate, giving the whole dish some substance: noodles, mashed potatoes, instant rice, wheat or pilaf. Then add whatever else is available in the way of goodies and yummies such as vegetable flakes, sauces or gravies. Some protein in the form of cheese or fish or meat. And finally, the seasoning that should turn the meal into a masterpiece (curry powder, for example, can transform the whole feeling of a one-pot dish). Don't forget plenty of salt, important in preventing cramps. This *pièce de résistance* is usually followed by a hot drink and/or a hot, often liquid dessert. (The finest is Royal powdered *flan*, available only in Argentina—so good luck.)

A good source of protein for such dinners is the lowly meat bar. Inedible raw, it's positively delicious when broken into a well-seasoned stew. A meat bar weighs 3 oz. (the equivalent of 16 oz. of raw meat) and provides 2700 calories per pound.

Everyone develops his own principles of winter camp cooking. The authors, for instance, find that freeze-dried dinners have a detestable pre-packaged taste to them. But we're crazy about olive oil and tomato paste in mountain stews, and almost addicted to *Kirschwasser* after a long day's skiing. In fact, even if you completely blow the dinner it will probably taste all right if you've skied hard enough. *Bon appetit!*

Most ski-touring chefs avoid pot cleaning at all cost, but this tendency is often countered by the pressing need to melt more water. The stove is never put aside till all the water bottles are filled and ready for the morning. It is sufficient to lay them between two sleeping bags to keep them from freezing.

WATER: This bugaboo is important enough to get a section all its own. On arriving at your campsite, the first thing you do is dispatch someone to look for water. If you can find free water, it will save untold trouble, fuel and time, and is well worth searching for.

If you've camped by an open stream—it's amazing at what cold temperatures one will find running water—it may take some ingenuity actually to collect the water. Tying a pot to a ski pole is often handy. If there is a fully covered stream, you may still be able to use it. On a recent tour in the Sierra we camped on a small meadow which one of the party recognized from summer. With the greatest scepticism we followed his directions in digging through fifteen feet of snow. But after much shoveling there it was, a beautiful patch of flowing water.

To melt snow on a stove, it's helpful to start with a little free water in the bottom of the pot before adding the snow—if you still have any in your water bottles. This speeds the initial melting and avoids the risk of scorching both pot and snow. Otherwise, press a small amount of snow into the bottom of the pot, and when this is wet add more snow. Powder snow takes forever to melt and many pots of snow are needed to produce one of water. If possible look for wet or soggy snow to speed the melting operation.

On sunny days a 'water machine' can be made from a

sheet of black plastic or dark nylon tarp. Place the sheet on
a slightly sloping surface and sprinkle snow onto it. The
melting water can be collected in a strategically placed pot
or wide-mouthed bottle. One can even bring half-gallon
plastic jugs along for storing water, but individual quart
bottles are handier during the day and less likely to freeze
at night.

The problem of dehydration on a ski tour is like the
problem of warmth. With common sense, there is no problem. Drink as often as you feel thirsty. And on the trail,
don't hesitate to eat snow, just warm it up in your mouth
to avoid chilling your stomach. Another good trick is to
refill a half-empty water bottle with snow after a rest stop,
and let it slosh around in your pack. At the next stop—a
full bottle again.

STOVES: On a long tour you depend on your stove as
much as on your tent or sleeping bag: no stove, no water.
The ideal skier's stove is light, stable, easy and foolproof to
operate.

For a group of four to six people, the most suitable
stoves are those with a *pump*, such as the Optimus 111B (B
for Benzine). This model has a one-pint capacity and burns
white-gas, an easier fuel to work with in cramped quarters
than kerosene. For two people, the Optimus 8R is adequate, but it has a small tank and no pump (thus requiring
priming). Stoves without pumps are temperamental and
often hard to start; and when they do start sometimes burn
with a disgustingly low flame. Both the 8R and the 111B
fold into a compact integral case which also serves as a
wide, flat, stable base. There are numerous other stoves,
however, which should be judged against these two popular
models.

A stove should be used on top of a small square pad of 1/8" ensolite to keep it from sinking into the snow. When cooking in a confined space (tent or cave) make sure there is adequate ventilation. Above all, learn the secrets of your stove. Even the most experienced mountaineers have lapses of intelligence. On one late spring tour, the authors and two of their friends were unable to light their stove for thirty hours because we used a 'backwards' starting procedure. We finally licked the problem by reading the directions printed on the stove.

Bluet-type butane cartridge stoves are very popular for short overnight tours, especially in spring when temperatures are not extremely cold. In the coldest weather they don't seem to have sufficient vapor pressure, and on long trips it is inefficient to carry the extra weight of individual cartridges.

Gasoline, for the traditional Optimus or Primus-type stove, is best carried in special fuel tins—flat-sided with two openings, a large one for filling the can, and a small one for pouring gas into the stove without a funnel. Be sure not to lose the cap gaskets or you will have fuel leaks. These can be disastrous, especially if the gas contaminates your food. It's probably safest to carry the fuel and the stove in outside pockets of your pack, as far away from the food as possible.

A safe quantity of fuel for a ski tour is around one and a quarter fillings per stove per day. An experienced party of four, with an Optimus 111B, will use about a pint of fuel per day, or slightly more if they have to melt a lot of powder snow.

COOKWARE: The best pots we have found are the aluminum nesting Swiss scout kettles, with dish-like covers and

wide bail handles. They come in four sizes, are light and
because of their rounded bottoms particularly easy to
clean. Two of these are adequate for any group up to six
people; the size of the pots depending on the number of
people. One pot is never enough, as snow and water must
be collected in something. A scrubbing pad and an extra
large cooking spoon complete the kit.

The best individual eating utensils we have found for
mountain trips are large measuring cups—the four-cup size
made of flexible plastic. They are easy to hold, easy to pour
from, don't freeze in the cold, and can be used as cups,
bowls and plates. (Metal cups and bowls are worthless.
Sometimes they freeze too cold to touch, yet full of hot
soup, they quickly become too hot to hold.) The large
plastic cup and a big spoon are all you need to enjoy
whatever good eats your party's collective imagination can
come up with.

Organizing the long tour

The key factor in the success of a long, multi-day tour is
neither the thoroughness of preparation nor the skiing
ability of the participants, but rather their ability to get
along and their commitment to the group effort. It's not
enough to trust your companions only in an emergency.
You must also be able to count on them to do their share
of all the minor chores that winter camping demands. And
to put up with all the potential irritations and frustrations
of heavy packs, awkward snow, cramped quarters and
minor aches and bruises, day after day after day. You have
to be moderately sure that you will still be friends after
three days in a tiny mountain tent or snow cave, waiting for

a storm to pass. In short, choosing the right party is half the battle.

Skiing skill can't be neglected. The further from civilization you go, the more critical it could be, as the possibility of outside help and ease of evacuation dwindle. For a long tour, it is essential that the members of the party have skied together before, and ideally they should have done a few short tours together.

Of course, under our general heading of multi-day ski tours, we find everything from a simple overnight trip to the month-long ski expedition. Overnight trips are an ideal shakedown to check out your equipment, organization, and the group's skiing level before undertaking anything more ambitious.

Basically, overnight trips are easy to organize and carry out. There's no need to modify the gear you use for day-tripping. Two days aren't long enough for you to worry about the nutritional balance of your food. The community gear (tent, food, pots, stove and gas) need not weigh much; so a few luxury extras, a few cans of fancy food or a bottle of wine, won't make you feel like a beast of burden. Our special comments will be directed, therefore, to skiers planning trips from four days to a week, or longer.

PURE CROSS-COUNTRY TRIPS: These are trips that don't involve climbing summits, or other mountaineering objectives. Some special problems are cutting weight to a minimum, modifying one's skiing gear for tougher conditions, and being ready to meet drastic changes in snow and weather en route.

Paradoxically, the more experienced you are, the less gear you take. After going over his equipment list to see if

he has everything, the seasoned tourer goes through it a
second time to see what he can possibly leave out. If your
personal gear represents the absolute minimum, then a lot
of odds and ends can be put in the community pile and a
certain duplication avoided. Why should everyone carry a
head lamp, a sewing kit, or a length of nylon utility cord in
his pack, when one will do very well for the whole group?

Food and gas for the stoves are almost impossible to
reduce in weight. But you can cache part of your supplies
in advance if your trip crosses a road, or follows the length
of a mountain mass with occasional side valleys and passes
offering access from 'civilization'. This is commonly done
by parties planning to ski sections of the John Muir trail in
the High Sierra, and in the Northern Sierra where there are
more access roads. It should be possible in many other areas
as well. An overnight trip to the cache point is well worth
it. For if you can break up a long ten-day tour into two
sections, you might cut the weight of your pack in half.
Traversing or cutting across a range the short way, there is
generally no way to cache food in advance; but these trips
seldom take more than a week, so the weight of the packs is
quite reasonable even though it slows you down. On long
trips in very remote regions, air-drops have been used with
great success, but these are more ski expeditions than ski
tours.

For trips longer than a couple of days, if you're a Nordic
skier, we suggest modifying your Nordic touring equipment. Heavier climbing boots and a flexible cable binding
(like the Silvretta) seem preferable to the low light Nordic
touring shoes and toe bindings. In pure Nordic ski-running
the feet never get cold. But large packs slow one to a walk,
and on sub-freezing days, light Nordic boots are not ade-

quate to keep your feet warm. Likewise, it's impossible to predict all the snow conditions you will encounter on a long trip. And the extra control afforded by side hitches on your cable bindings could be helpful traversing icy slopes, as well as on the descent. Finally, the more expensive Nordic skis (of fiberglass and compound construction) are often preferable for long tours, because of their light weight and extreme strength. (The tips are almost unbreakable.) A broken ski might be repaired with a plastic ski tip; but if your skis really shattered, you might find yourself walking out. This is one more reason for preferring a heavy mountain boot, which won't really hamper your skiing that much.

And on long trips, sudden changes of weather and conditions can cause you to make drastic changes in the planned route of your tour. Most long tours involve crossing a few passes or ridges connecting two valleys; these passes are generally the steepest pitches, and can be rendered impassable from new snow and high avalanche risk. It's best to have considered this possibility beforehand and to have made a tentative decision about what you would do. If there are alternative routes at a lower angle, you can find them on your maps before leaving. If there are none, you may have to sit tight in camp for a day or two, waiting for the snow to settle and avalanche risk to reduce. Even this alternative needs advance planning, as you must have a few extra days' food or a good idea of how to stretch your rations. In short, the more cut-off you are, the more prepared you have to be. This is both the major headache and the great attraction of long ski trips.

SKI-MOUNTAINEERING TRIPS: The worlds of the mountain climber and the skier naturally overlap. But in America, more often than not, climbers have regarded skiing with a hostile mixture of disapproval and contempt. Too proud of their own rugged scene to spend the time needed to master what they consider a sissy and commercialized sport, climbers have assumed that snowshoes were the ideal means of over-the-snow transportation for expeditions to remote high ranges. (Until recently, there hasn't been much serious winter climbing in this country). Needless to say, we disagree. In fact, for a number of reasons, skis are the most efficient means a climber can use for getting to and from his peak, and sometimes part way up it, in a winter setting.

This is especially true of high-altitude expeditions, where one must ascend glacial slopes day after day, as on the typical Alaskan expedition. The combination of climbing equipment, and the usual camping gear and food, results in too much weight for the party to carry at one go. So it's necessary to resort to ferrying or relaying loads. On skis, one can adopt a ferrying system that allows the party to 'carry high and sleep low' (the most desirable strategy for acclimatizing to higher altitudes), and yet do a full day's packing upward each day.

Tents and sleeping gear are left behind; and the team carries other supplies upward all day, caching them in the evening at the highest point. They can then descend on skis in a matter of minutes or, say, an hour, the route that took all day to ascend. After sleeping at the low camp, the remaining gear, tents, etc. can be moved up to the cache and a new camp established. It's obvious that on snowshoes, the descent to get the next load would take approximately as long as the climb. This would mean ferrying half the distance, or sleeping at the upper cache—which might involve a double set of tents, and in any case would not be ideal for acclimatization.

Of course, it's vital to mark the cache of loads in a permanently visible way: long bamboo wands and banners are good. And if the glacial terrain is flat and featureless, it's not a bad idea to place small wands along the trail you may have to descend in evening fog. Once in an Alaskan fog, we had to snowplow seven miles down a glacier, staring between our ski tips at the faint white traces of our ascent —just because we'd neglected this obvious marking procedure.

Another reason we like skis for high mountain travel is their safety on a crevassed glacier. Skis spread one's weight as widely as possible on potentially fragile snow bridges across crevasses. If you're actually sliding at the moment you cross a crevasse (always perpendicularly), your speed will further decrease the dynamic loading and reduce the stress you put on the sometimes flimsy snow bridge.

We once followed the tracks of a snowshoeing party through a twisting, heavily-crevassed ice-fall. We counted four separate holes where the other party had broken through thin snowbridges, but we passed without incident on our skis. Of course, we, too, were roped up. Roped skiing, and crevasse rescue techniques, are covered in detail in chapter 10, but this is a good time for a warning. You're not likely to break through a snow bridge on skis, but should you do so, *there's blue eternity down below unless you're roped up*. Unroped skiing is so much easier, and so much fun, that there's a great temptation just to let the last man carry the rope in his pack. This is all right if the snow bridges are thick, and the party consists of good skiers unlikely to fall in the center of a snow bridge. But you must assess the danger, make a decision, and then suffer the consequences. Skiing by yourself on a glacier is utter folly, as Louis Lachenal, one of the greatest French alpinists, discovered on the easy *Mer de Glace* run. The classic photo of the Lachenal tragedy, two ski tracks dead-ending in a small dark hole, is sobering indeed.

On a big mountain, another problem that becomes critical is that of keeping your boots dry. No matter how much you've 'sno-sealed' your boots, they still get damp after a long day on slushy, sun-warmed glacier snow. The problem is that they don't dry out at night. And as you progress up the mountain, colder conditions will freeze the water-impregnated leather during the day, with consequences ranging from cold feet to frostbite. Waterproof overboots are the ideal answer. They don't seem to interfere with the functioning of cable or step-in touring bindings, and can be worn around camp with down booties inside for real comfort. Overboots aren't necessary for most lowland trips, or for overnight touring; but day after day at high altitudes, gaiters just don't seem sufficient.

There are a few other helpful tactics for high-mountain skiing—such as using tents for a quick one-night camp, but still building an ice-cave or igloo when you have to hole up for a few days in bad weather. Basically, though it's no different than any other kind of touring. You apply the same technique with common-sense variations. For shorter ski mountaineering trips in the 'home ranges,' there's little or nothing to add.

For winter or spring mountaineers, or summer explorers of distant snowy ranges, the effort expended in learning to ski will be amply rewarded in greater mobility and consequently a greater likelihood of making your peak. Climbing a peak on skis, just for the run down, is also a form of ski mountaineering. But aside from a little extra caution with cornices along a summit ridge, there are no special procedures to stress. You should always be prepared for more challenging skiing, when the quest for a peak takes you above timberline. Here wind and sun vent their force unchecked; and wind-crusted and sun-slabbed snow is quite common near the summits of Alpine peaks. There's always a challenge.

Part II.
The Wilderness Skier's Environment and its Hazards

6. Mountains In Winter

This is the chapter we almost left out of the book. To the experienced wilderness skier or mountain traveler, most of what we will cover is old hat—information acquired so long ago that is has become automatic, obvious mountain truths reduced to the level of offhand clichés.

Nonetheless, for a beginner, especially a newcomer to the Alpine zones of our western peaks, a pocket guide to the mountain landscape may be helpful. We've already noted that the Nordic skier who remains below timberline, skiing on open rolling sub-alpine terrain, faces a less hostile and less complex (though no less beautiful) environment. For this reason we will concentrate on what might be called the high mountain landscape. (For a more general and more thorough coverage of mountain geography and topography, we recommend reading the appropriate chapters of *Mountaineering, the Freedom of the Hills* by the Seattle Mountaineers. For great detail on the subtleties of compass navigation and its theory, we recommend *Be Expert with Map and Compass* by Bjorn Kjellstrom. For a fine general treatment of mountain weather, read the chapter on weather in *Freedom of the Hills*.

The shape of mountains

Here we will stress what each mountain feature means to the skier. And thus we overlap, inevitably, the subjects of orientation and avalanche danger. But that's the way it is in the mountains.

Ascending from lower elevations toward the high peaks,

the wilderness skier will encounter in rough succession the
following mountain features and their special challenges.

FORESTS AND LAKES: Illogically, we dump forests and
lakes into the same section, merely because they are found
at low altitudes in flat country, as well as on steeper higher
terrain.

Forested areas are generally more attractive to Nordic
than to Alpine skiers. They vary greatly in density and
problems—as you will discover after a few experiences.
Dense stands of timber and thick brush are almost impen-
etrable on skis. And even in more open woods, 'hang ups'
and hidden traps abound. The worst are fallen logs and
down timber along your route. When lightly covered with
snow, these can stop you cold, or make you pitch forward
on your face, should you run into them unprepared. The
best technique is to advance one ski and weight your heels;
this usually lets you slide over half-buried obstacles in good
balance. Of course, if you're walking (not gliding) on your
skis, there is no problem. But, even worse than logs are
individual branches buried beneath the snow, which can
trap only your ankles, producing a serious fall if you're
moving fast. The sole defense against these invisible obstacles is to recognize where they are likely to be found (a
matter of experience). In general, avoid skiing next to trees
if you're moving fast. This also keeps you away from the
deep circular moats which can form around the base of
trees in certain conditions.

The biggest practical problem, however, is route finding.
When you've seen one tree, you've seen them all. So don't
count on landmarks in a dense forest. Try to use everything
external to the forest itself as guides: ridges, distant peaks,

rivers, and the general slope of the ground. Fortunately, popular touring trails in forested areas generally get marked—with some kind of blaze, or painted tin trail-markers nailed high up on trees—after a few parties have lost their way. Dense flat forests, along with featureless flat glaciers, are the only situations we can think of where a compass is probably essential.

Lakes in the snow country, surprisingly enough, offer fine skiing most of the winter and well into spring. But an image of breaking ice will always cross your mind as you ski out onto a frozen lake. Elementary prudence is in order. Unless you know without doubt how thick the ice is, space the party out at wide intervals. Ask yourself whether you could take off your skis and your pack, should you break through and find yourself in the water. If the answer is no, then do something about it—loosen packstraps, undo arlberg straps and pole straps.

The ice at the edge of a well-frozen lake is often thin and slushy. Don't let this freak you out. But in any case, test the ice with your ski pole before venturing out. While covered with a deep blanket of snow, most lakes are quite safe to ski on. Sometimes in spring, however, the lake starts to look suspicious; it no longer feels solid. In this case, as elsewhere, you must trust your instinct. If you don't feel right about it, don't cross a frozen lake. Large blue cracks in the surface are, of course, a definite *no* signal.

VALLEYS AND CANYONS: In Alpine valleys, infinite in variety, the skier generally follows a stream or river bed. Or else, he skis along the flatter benches found above the stream level. Sometimes large willows or other tall under-brush make it impossible actually to follow a stream, even in winter. But the stream, along with the ridge-lines on either side of the valley, are your main guides in navigating. Alpine valleys are often stepped into a series of lower-angled valleys separated by steep headwalls. These headwalls, which are often talus slopes in summer, demand a little thought. They're usually ascended by zig-zagging; although on frozen spring snow, it's easier to carry one's skis and kick steps directly up the slope. Even below timber line, these headwalls provide open slopes, ideal for linked turns on the descent.

Hanging valleys are small, and usually situated high above (and to the side of) a larger main valley. Hanging valleys are connected to the main valley by steep slopes, precipitous watercourses, or small steep canyons which are often blocked by cliff bands. It's usually a tough climb to get into a hanging valley; and the slopes beneath it may well be potential avalanche sites.

Steep narrow valleys, or canyons, must be treated with respect and a certain suspicion by skiers. They often have sides of slabby rock which provide an insecure anchorage for snow. And even if canyons are perfectly safe when you pass on the ascent, they can become real avalanche traps if you have to descend them after an intervening snowfall. (On a multi-day tour, for example.) Likewise, it's very difficult to pick a gradual and non-fatiguing route up a steep-sided canyon.

RIDGES AND GULLIES: Where there are valleys there will be ridges above; and these are quite important to the wilderness skier. In areas with high avalanche hazard, ridges are theoretically the safest routes of travel. (But in fact, precipitous, twisting Alpine ridges, at higher elevations, are often impossible routes. Paradoxically, these 'safe' ridges are hazardous because of their cornices).

Cornices are the typical overhanging snow formations, deposited on the lee (or protected) side of a ridge by the wind. (See fig. 26.) The same wind that builds a cornice tends to deposit a slab-like layer of snow, or 'scarp,' beneath the cornice. The scarp is prone to avalanching. A collapsing cornice can trigger an avalanche, too. Or it can drop the unwary skier suddenly onto the slope below. A cornice collapsing beneath you is always disagreeable, generally serious, and sometimes fatal. So treat all cornices with respect.

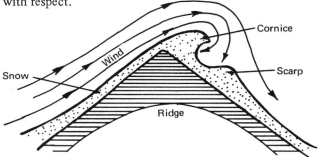

Fig. 26. How Cornices Are Formed

They are not all death traps, however. Jumping off a vertical-to-overhanging cornice, landing in balance and swinging into a perfect series of short turns—this is one of the ultimate joys of skiing. The main problem is judging the size of the overhang, and the stability of the cornice, from above. Try to get a side view. And approach the edge very gingerly, whacking at the snow with an outstretched pole.

But if you don't actually want to ski off a cornice, it's better to stay away from the crest altogether.

Of interest to the skier is the fact that snow conditions are almost never the same on both sides of a ridge. Each slope will have a different sun-orientation, as well as a different relation to the prevailing winds. One side of a ridge may offer great skiing while the opposite side is virtually unskiable. Or in a more favorable case, one face of a ridge may offer a hard wind-blown surface, ideal for climbing; and on the other side you will find undisturbed deep powder for a perfect descent. The same must be said of passes between two watersheds.

Gullies, or couloirs (narrow, steep, funnel-like gullies), generally drop down from the crest of a ridge—though both can be found in the middle of a mountain face. Gullies are classical avalanche lines: extremely dangerous because they channel snow during an avalanche, so that it piles up deeper and deeper. But gullies and couloirs also provide very good, if challenging, downhill skiing. And very often they are the only skiing routes through a rocky face or a cliff band. The special ski technique needed in order to ski extremely steep couloirs and snow faces are covered in chapter 10, under 'extreme skiing.'

For the average skier, gullies and couloirs are generally a problem. They do not lend themselves to zig-zag traversing, either up or down. So you are often obliged to remove your skis and walk up, or down—or else traverse onward, looking for more suitable terrain. If you must follow a gully when the snow seems unstable, or when there is danger of rock-fall from above, avoid the middle and stay on the sides. Even crossing a gully can be dangerous in certain conditions. A party should cross one man at a time, and as fast as possible. In a winter snowstorm, steep couloirs can become veritable synchronized funnels for continued spindrift avalanches, or light powder avalanches. Curiously, you can time the interval between these avalanches—whose regular build-up and release depends on the rate the snow is falling —and dash across between two of them. But logically, you shouldn't find yourself in such a situation on a ski tour.

GLACIAL FEATURES: As he seeks out higher peaks and longer runs, the wilderness skier eventually encounters glaciers. A glacier is really nothing more than a large, permanent body of fully compacted snow—that is, ice. Through their erosive and rock-transporting action, glaciers have sculpted much of the relief of the typical mountain range. As a skier climbs up onto a glacier he will encounter, in roughly this order, the following features.

Moraines. These are the large rims, or ridges of boulders, that mark the lowest limit of the glacier's advance. Since most glaciers are now in retreat, moraines are often found far below the actual glacier—and often in valleys where the glacier itself disappeared ages ago. So moraines are just steep boulder-covered hills, barring your progress up or down a valley. If the snow cover is thin, unstable talus blocks beneath may give you a lot of trouble. But generally you just climb over them and keep going. A moraine just below a glacier is a *terminal moraine.*

The *glacial tongue* or *snout.* This is the bottom edge of the glacier. If it is steep, overhanging, or shattered by crevasses, you probably have no business there on skis— you'll have to go around, following the side or *lateral moraines.*

Crevasses. These are the cracks, from miniscule to gigantic—some are 50 feet across and two hundred feet deep, or more—that split the smooth surface of a glacier. Glacier ice is more or less solid and brittle. But the whole glacier behaves in a plastic manner, flowing slowly downhill like a frozen white river. The stresses and deformations produced by this flow—both downhill over irregular terrain, and around corners—cause crevasses to appear. They tend to run across the glacier, perpendicular to its direction of flow, although sometimes exceptions to this rule are in the majority. Crevasses, in turn, are in constant, though invisible, flux. They open further, or are compressed or distorted from year to year. Nor do they always present the same obstacle to the ski mountaineer. In midwinter, crevasses may be solidly bridged though hidden from sight. In summer, open crevasses on a 'dry' glacier may be impossible to pass, yet safe, because they are completely visible. The in-between conditions are the trickiest, and the most dangerous.

In selecting a route up or down a glacier, it's important to pick out areas with the fewest crevasses. Crevasses are most numerous where the glacier passes over a drop off, or a convex slope. Likewise, they will be numerous on the outside of a bend in the glacier. These large numbers of crevasses are produced by tension, or outward buckling of the ice mass, flowing over or around an obstacle. The opposite force, compression, reduces the number of crevasses on the inside of a bend in the glacier, or concave dip in the glacier's surface.

Crevasses are an obstacle to route-finding, and a major hazard for the mountain skier. Techniques for roped skiing on glaciers, and crevasse rescue, are discussed at length in chapter 10. One problem here is the lack of precise rules.

It's all very well to say: 'Never ski unroped on a glacier.' But everyone, including the authors, breaks this rule. Skis, we've already pointed out, make it safer to cross snow bridges over crevasses. But all snow bridges should be regarded with suspicion at first.

A glacier may also have other esoteric features. An *ice fall* is created when the glacier literally 'falls' over a steep cliff or slope. These are chaotic jumbles of crevasses, broken debris, ice cliffs and ice towers, called *seracs*. (In European usage, a *serac* is any ice cliff that overhangs a snow or ice slope.)

At the top of the glacier, dividing it from the snowfields above, we find a large crevasse called in French a *rimaye*, and in German and English the *bergschrund*. Above the bergschrund are permanent fields of consolidated (*firn* or *neve*) snow which 'feed' the glacier year after year. If the glacier dead-ends against a peak or peaks, snow couloirs dropping from these peaks will likewise be separated from the main glacier by a *bergschrund*. If you are continuing upward, you will find that crossing the bergschrund can be a real task—generally one must employ some of the special mountaineering techniques described in chapter 10.

Hanging glaciers, as opposed to the more normal valley glaciers, are small glaciers perched high on the flanks of large peaks. They generally end in ice cliffs, from which periodic avalanches of falling blocks can threaten the terrain, or a party, below.

In the continental United States, ski touring on glaciers is a relatively infrequent thing. And the glaciers themselves are quite small. Of course, in winter, the brutal distinction between the ice of a glacier, and the rocky terrain beneath, is all but erased by a blanket of snow. Without actually being on a proper glacier, you often feel yourself in a glacial setting: esthetic exhilaration without objective danger. When skiing the wilderness mountains of Western Canada and Alaska, however, glacier travel and its hazards are common.

HIGH-MOUNTAIN TERRAIN: Aside from a few couloirs, and steep faces of hard *neve* or *firn* snow, skiable snow slopes seldom extend higher than the highest glaciers of a given region. Of course, there are mountains with wide rounded ridges, not-too-steep faces, and an overall friendly appearance, which are completely covered with snow and offer good skiing from the very summit all the way down— possibly passing through a lower glacial zone. But often, the highest snowy faces of major peaks are simply too steep to be skiable.

There is, in fact, no way to generalize about the shape or form of a high mountain peak. We will just give a list of typical features—more important to the mountaineer than to the skier, as they concern rock, or mixed terrain, rather than snow—and try to define some of the more esoteric high-mountain terminology.

Buttresses are abrupt steep ridges, of snow or rock or both; or they may be steep 'steps' in a long ridge. On high-mountain ridges, we often find pinnacles or a series of small sharp pinnacles called *gendarmes*—these bar your way like a hostile French policeman. A narrow or 'knife-edged' ridge is referred to as an *arête*.

The small passes leading from one side of a mountain ridge to the other are referred to as *saddles* or *cols*. And very small passes between two pinnacles, or between a pinnacle and the mountain proper, are called *notches*.

Gullies and *couloirs*, already mentioned, are just as often found high on a major peak as on lower ridges. They need not be filled with snow, but can be pure rock—and they often provide logical lines of ascent. Very small steep couloirs with parallel walls, called *chimneys*, also provide obvious routes for the climber. They are ascended with a thousand-and-one variations on the time-honored technique of jamming one's body inside, and pushing, grunting and inching, i.e. *chimneying*, one's way up.

In general, climbing routes up a steep or complex mountain tend to follow the obvious lines of least resistance. These are ridges, sloping ledge-systems or *ramps*, gullies, couloirs and chimneys. The evolution of alpinism over the years has brought us to the period of the *directissima*; where leading climbers seek out the most brutal and direct lines up the steepest, least hospitable faces. But this spirit is an extreme one, and really has little bearing on general winter mountaineering, or the casual 'peak-bagging' which can be such an enjoyable part of a ski tour.

One often hears the expression, *summit ridge*, which is self-explanatory, and this brings us to the top or summit of our imaginary peak. Traditionally, one finds a pile of rocks —a cairn—left as an ego-monument to the first-ascent party. But in winter, this is often mercifully buried under the snow. Don't bother to dig it up. The mountain itself should be enough.

Finally, an area of related summits is a *range*, a *massif*, or a *group* of peaks. A mountain valley or basin ringed about by mountains is referred to as a *cirque* of peaks. So much for mountain features, Now, how do we find our way through them?

Orientation

It is our somewhat heretical feeling that a 'sense of the landscape,' a good pair of eyes, common sense and a map—but not necessarily a compass—are the basic tools for orientation and navigation on a wilderness ski trip. On a recent trans-Alpine tour, a successful German party skied over 2,000 kilometers and used about 200 maps but didn't even carry a compass.

We're not suggesting you leave the compass out, or that you shouldn't learn to use it well. In fact, you can have a lot of fun with a compass on a ski tour. But it is unrealistic to count on using 'compass navigation' to find your way around in a storm or in a whiteout. The primary rule for navigating blind is—don't. In exceptional circumstances, of course, you may have to anyway. But nine times out of ten, it's better to wait for the period of extreme low visibility to pass. Storms sometimes last for days, but whiteouts almost never do. Increasing and critical avalanche danger, for instance, might spur you on to travel in conditions where visual orientation is impossible. But by that time you're in real trouble anyway. If we had to choose, we would take a good bivouac sack before a compass any day.

The same applies to travel at night. If there's a moon out, navigation is no different than daytime; and the skiing can be far more beautiful. But simply pressing on at night, is a very risky business. If you're trying to ski downhill, you can easily get hurt. Even headlamps aren't adequate. Nor will the tunnel of light from your lamps help you pick out blazes high on trees, or spot any of the peripheral landmarks so important to real ski navigation. Once again, the best answer is usually to stay put, settle in, and keep going in the morning.

Having said all this, however, we still recommend that the serious wilderness skier take a topographic map and compass most of the time. Just recognize their limits, and your own. Excellent topographic maps, of virtually every mountain or touring area in North America, are readily available. Get them from your local hiking, backpacking, climbing or ski shop; or by writing directly to the *Map Information Office, U.S. Geological Survey, Washington, D.C. 20242.* The use of these maps, the function of contour lines, the importance of local magnetic declination etc., are described in so many other texts, that we will skip these basics and mention only points of importance to the skier.

Of major importance is your skill in rapidly visualizing terrain, when looking at contour lines on a map. You should be able to see at a glance whether a series of 'vees' represent a ridge line or a gully, without puzzling over it and looking around to check altitudes. Likewise, you must learn to recognize features important to the skier, such as a more-or-less level bench contouring an otherwise steep hillside. Be aware, too, of the limitations of even the most detailed topographic maps. They indicate only ground contour but not where you will find snow, nor how deep that snow will be. In areas of high snow-depth and frequent slide activity, the small-scale contour of the terrain can change radically, although the large-scale features stay the same. Photographs, taken at roughly the same season as your tour, can be an invaluable aid in 'doping out' the snow-covered landscape.

The first thing one does with the map is orient it, that is, line it up with visible landmarks. If you don't recognize any landmarks, use the compass to align the map. Only then can you attempt to spot landmarks, and learn the terrain, by reference to the map. In any case, the important thing is to use the map to build up your picture and feeling for the terrain. Don't attempt to follow slavishly a pre-determined penciled-in route.

If you simply don't know where you are, you can reestablish your exact position with the compass by taking a heading (or compass direction) from two known landmarks, and plotting these two lines on the map. (A compass attached to a plastic square is useful for this.) Your position is found at the intersection of the two lines. Even just one sighting can give a lot of information, if you are on (or near) some longish landmark like a stream or a ridge identifiable on the map. Your position is roughly where the line from your single sighting intersects the stream or ridge.

But if you're really lost, if you don't know where you are and can't spot any major landmarks—then map and compass can provide only vague suggestions, not concrete answers. Some known data is a must for proper navigation. At this point you will, in fact, be dealing less with navigation than with general mountain strategy. What do you do? Stay cool, consider the alternatives, and make what seems the most reasonable decision. Either follow your tracks back to some known point, or use the general lay of the land to guide you somewhere else where accurate orientation will be possible. For instance, if you know what valley or watershed you're in, you're seldom really lost. You can follow the valley upward to a known pass, or down to the confluence of a couple of creeks. Not knowing exactly where you are is a long way from really being lost.

Your map will obviously be consulted every time you cross a pass or enter a new watershed with a new vista. Use it to learn the country. Perhaps the most pleasant use for your map is to carry it to a summit, and then consult it to

identify distant features on the horizon which would otherwise remain anonymous, uninteresting peaks. Altogether,
orientations, route-finding and navigation aren't such buga-
boos as they are often made out to be. As boy scouts we
used to make these subjects very complicated, because that
was part of the game. But the adventure itself has become
more complex and more real since those days; the details
must be kept simple. The complete wilderness skier actually
feels at home in these winter woods or peaks. In order for
you to feel at home here, you'll have to build up a real
sixth sense about orientation, which can only come from a
lot of ski touring.

Winter weather

Even the professional meteorologist is often baffled by the
local vagaries of mountain weather. Yet this weather is
doubly important to the wilderness skier. It affects not
only the skier himself—scorching, soaking or freezing him—
but also the snow he skis on. A sudden weather change can
double the effective length of your tour, or even render it
impossible.

If you ski a great deal in one area, however, you can
develop an amazing sense of what the weather will do. For
example, in the northern High Sierra of California, we've
learned not to take bad weather signs too seriously unless
they are preceded by a day or two of violent winds. In the
central Sierra, on the other hand, strong winds tend to
follow, not precede, a major storm. It's not entirely logical,
but there it is. Similar rules of thumb for outguessing the
weather will be collected by anyone who really knows his
'home' mountains.

Sudden weather changes are easy to cope with on a short tour (anyway, one doesn't usually go on a one-day excursion unless the weather looks good). The critical problem is figuring out what the weather will do once you're embarked on a long ski trip. Bad weather signs are legion: rising wind, cloud build-up, dramatic temperature changes, etc. Are these the signs of a local weather disturbance which may last only a few hours? Or is this a major frontal system moving through—which could bring long-range weather changes lasting for days? Alas, sometimes there isn't any way to tell.

High thin cirrus clouds, formed of ice crystals, are classical warnings of the arrival of a warm front. And bad weather from warm fronts tends to last longer than the shorter, more violent storms due to passing cold fronts. A falling barometer is always bad news. The ski mountaineer can get a lot of use out of a pocket or wrist-watch altimeter, which doubles as a barometer. But remember to read it in the opposite sense, that is, rising altimeter means falling barometer. Lens-shaped or lenticular clouds are absolute signs of serious bad weather in some areas (e.g. the 'cap' on the Aiguille Verte), and absolutely meaningless in others. Finally, a weather pattern that seems to deteriorate more each day, for several days in a row, is usually a sign that you'll be hit by something big.

Small-scale or local weather is not to be laughed at, but is generally less serious. The spring skier will encounter a lot of afternoon cloud build-up and, occasionally, the daily thunderstorms and lightning more typical of early summer. Here too, long standing local experience is the best guide.

But if it's difficult to second-guess tomorrow's weather, it's almost always possible to find out what the weather has been like for a week or so before you start your tour. This information will tell you a lot about the snow conditions before you even get started. In springtime, it's especially important to find out if the snow has been freezing well at night—if not, your skiing could be ruined by slushy snow at 8:00 a.m. and unskiable glop by noon. For this information, as well as advice on potential avalanche hazard, your best source is a Forest Service or National Park ranger (or warden in Canada). Keeping track of such things is their job, but not enough skiers take advantage of this ready expertise.

What other sources of weather information are there besides the evening news? If you have a friend who is a licensed private pilot, get him to explain the mysterious workings of the Flight Service Station network. And, just before leaving, have him get you their long range forecast for the region you want to visit. These FSS's have the most accurate, up-to-date weather information we have yet found anywhere. Theirs is, however, a service for pilots—so don't abuse it.

So much for our quick glance at winter weather. We are all too aware that far from doing it justice, we have scarcely gotten damp. But in the mountains, a common-sense approach to weather will serve you as well as a scientific one. Be prepared for grim weather and it won't bother you so much. If you're unprepared, it can be a killer. And remember, too, that storms and bad weather are not the skier's only concern. The overall weather pattern of a given winter, as well as any sudden weather changes, can have important consequences for the wilderness skier as we shall see in the following chapter on snow and avalanches.

7. Snow and Avalanches

If the medium is the message, then snow has a very particular message for the wilderness skier. Snow is everything: source of the skier's pleasures, frustrations and dangers. Friend or foe, but almost never neutral. Snow is not just a part of the wilderness skier's world, it is that world.

Yet very few skiers really know much about snow. Because of the intricacies of waxing, most Nordic skiers are far more snow-conscious than Alpine skiers. (Of course, once a ski run has been packed, it's just the same old white playground.) Yet in a sense, the Alpine touring skier needs to understand snow even more than the Nordic skier, since he will be skiing and crossing steeper and potentially more dangerous slopes. He must not only know the qualities of a given snow surface, but also be able to guess its buried secrets.

To understand snow and avalanches, a certain amount of basic theory is necessary. This is where the average reader or skier gets lost: a complete explanation of the mechanical, thermal and dynamic properties of the snow cover is heavy reading at best. For this reason, we've tried to simplify our snow theory as much as possible. The last part of this chapter, on practical measures for dealing with avalanche hazard is the most important. Don't just read it. Think about it a little afterwards.

The story of snow

Snow reaches the earth in millions of tiny crystals. It accumulates in blanket-like layers or strata. And from the

moment it is deposited, it is always undergoing some process of change.

The classical stellar snow crystal (a hexagonal star, called
a dendrite) is the best-known form, but represents only one
end of a whole spectrum. Other types of snow crystals,
including plates, rods, needle crystals and rounded pellet-
like snow called graupel, are generally denser than the light
powder snow composed of star-shaped crystals. The lightest
snow will fall in very cold windless conditions; the densest,
when the temperature is 'warm' (around the freezing
point). The action of wind on falling snow can also result in
more densely packed snow—since the delicate branches of
the crystals are broken off or damaged by the wind, permitting them to settle and bond, or become packed closer
together. This important phenomenon is called age hardening, and is a common agent of slab formation.

Once new snow is deposited, each crystal begins to
undergo a process of change and transformation. This metamorphism as it is called (with the specialist's usual disregard
for the common forms of speech) involves sublimation—the
changing of ice to water vapor, and back to ice, without
passing through a liquid water phase. (In fact, snow crystals
are formed in the atmosphere by a process of sublimation.)
Once on the ground, sublimation and re-sublimation take
ice from the crystal arms, branches or ends, and redeposit it
near the center of the snow crystal. Thus the snow crystal
itself is reduced in size, becoming more dense. Consequently, a snow layer consisting of these metamorphosing crystals keeps slowly settling and compressing under its own
weight, or the weight of new snow above. In this way, one
foot of new snow can be reduced to 8 inches in a day or so,
without actually melting. This is what Nordic skiers refer to

as settled snow. This type of metamorphism, which actually consolidates the snow cover, is perversely named destructive metamorphism, since the individual snow crystals are being broken down.

Settling and compacting, either from destructive metamorphism or from excess weight of snow, allows the crystals to bond together better, and to form more-or-less cohesive layers of snow. The bonding within a single layer of snow (all deposited at one time) is almost always better than the bonding between two distinct layers of snow; although that too can also be quite strong. Thus, a history of winter weather is left in the snow cover by different layers representing different storms (or breaks within a storm), and by different stages of snow transformation within each layer.

Not all change or metamorphism leads to more compact snow. One process in particular can drastically weaken a snow layer, and this is called, with equal perversity, constructive metamorphism. It works as follows. Snow is a moderately good insulator. Thus, no matter how cold the winter air, a covering of snow will keep the ground layer around 32° F. (the freezing point). But higher up in the snow, closer to the surface, the temperature may be a good deal colder. When the snow cover is shallow, and the air extremely cold, such differences in temperature (temperature gradients) can become quite abrupt. This increases the upward sublimation of water vapor, redepositing it as ice on a higher level of crystals—and building them up in size until they become large cup-shaped crystals with low adherence to one another. A layer of such metamorphosed cup crystals always appears loose and non-cohesive, and is popularly called 'sugar snow,' or more precisely depth hoar.

Depth hoar is most typically formed early in winter—due to thin snow cover and cold temperatures—and is particularly common in the Rockies. It is one of the most unstable layers possible within the snow cover; and once formed, has a direct bearing on later avalanche hazard. Unfortunately, there's no off-hand way to know whether a weak layer of depth hoar is present beneath the snow surface. Only periodic observations of snowfall and weather patterns throughout the winter can give insight into such mysteries. (Forest Service avalanche personnel and ski patrol leaders have such information, and later we'll see how to use it.)

A similar but inverse temperature gradient (when the snow surface is colder than the air) can produce small frost feathers or crystals of surface hoar overnight. These usually melt during the day. But if they grow fairly large and are then buried by new snow, they can constitute another weak or unstable layer in the snow.

From a pragmatic point of view, any unstable layer in the snow is of great importance to the skier—either non-cohesive snow that won't resist weight and stress; or else snow layers to which other, new-snow layers cannot bond strongly. Such layers might be a sun-crusted surface or (worse yet) a rain-crust on top of old snow. In fact, no icy surface will offer a good bond to new snow. Nor will a loose, unconsolidated layer of dry powder or 'wild' snow. Somewhat consolidated, somewhat rough, and somewhat porous surfaces provide the best bonding for additional layers of snow. But the character of the new layer is equally important. If the new snowfall starts wet and becomes drier, bonding to the old snow will be better than in the reverse case.

Finally, the whole snow cover is subject to one last kind

of metamorphism, melt metamorphism. This leads to spring or corn snow, and the formation of large stable summer-snowfields (or *nevés*) above glaciers. Melt metamorphism involves melting and re-freezing, rather than sublimation. It forms the granular snow crystals that make spring skiing in the high mountains such a delight. This is the sort of snow on which Nordic skiers use their klister waxes; it is referred to in some waxing charts as old snow, or in a loose way, metamorphosed snow. Eventually melt metamorphism plus pressure will turn spring snow (or *nevé* or *firnschnee*) into true glacier ice.

So much for the transformation of snow. But the snow cover as a whole has certain properties which are very important in understanding avalanches. Snow can behave almost like a very thick gooey liquid, or a somewhat soft elastic solid: it is a *visco-elastic* material. The warmer the snow, the higher its viscosity: that is, the more it will flow, give and deform. Conversely, the colder it is the more brittle the snow mass or its layers will become. These properties are important in understanding what happens to snow on a hill, its motion and the forces within it.

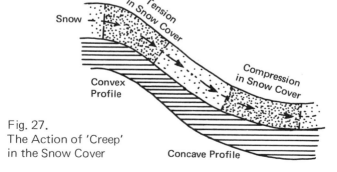

Fig. 27.
The Action of 'Creep' in the Snow Cover

When snow is lying on a flat surface it will settle under the influence of destructive metamorphism and gravity. On a slope, one component of gravity is always pulling the snow mass down the hill. And so the settling action becomes 'creep'—a slow downward flow or deformation of the snow. (If the snow mass is not solidly anchored to the ground, the same force may even produce a 'glide' of the whole snow cover along the ground.)

The slow and often imperceptible creep of the snow cover down the hill produces forces or stresses within the snow. On a convex profile (slope bulging or dropping steeply away) the snow is under tension, or stretched. On a concave profile (hollow or decreasing slope) the snow is under compression. Tension in the snow cover on a convex slope is particularly important. Part of the snow is trying to pull away from itself, and it is here that we expect (and find) trigger points, or fracture lines for slab avalanches. Speaking very roughly, the warmer the snow, the more it can 'give' and adjust to these stresses. In colder snow, mechanical stress will remain present and unequalized for longer periods.

Avalanche theory

Avalanche study is such a complex field that it seems pretentious even to speak of avalanche theory. Here we only hope to cover the main types of avalanches, and explain roughly how they happen. The non-theoretical aspects—practical measures for the wilderness skier—will be discussed in the next section.

What causes an avalanche? Basically, a quantity of snow gets too heavy for whatever is holding it up and slides away.

An avalanche is released when the sliding stress (that weight of snow acting parallel to the slope) becomes greater than the strength of whatever is anchoring the snow. Or, an avalanche may be released when the strength (or resistance to sliding) of whatever anchors the snow is somehow reduced. When an avalanche is triggered by an external force, like a skier, what has really happened is this: the forces involved have been disturbed and redistributed, so that the final balance is not enough to hold the snow in place.

There are two main types of snow avalanche: *loose snow avalanches* and *slab avalanches*. Loose snow avalanches start at a point and fan out. The loose snow involved is non-cohesive, so that a given crystal is held in place mostly by friction against other crystals. When the snow piles up past its natural angle of repose, a few crystals slump downward; and once a little snow starts moving, a sort of chain reaction takes place. (Moving friction is always less than static friction, so after a critically poised area of snow has moved, it tends to keep on sliding.)

Slab avalanches are more complex, and represent a greater hazard, especially for the skier. In a slab avalanche, a large area of snow begins to slide at once. The snow is cohesive to some degree, and has been effectively anchored to the slope as a whole unit or 'slab' of snow. Before looking at the two important sub-divisions, soft slab and hard slab avalanches, we should ask: What anchors a slab of snow?

The primary and strongest anchorage of any slab (or compacted well-bonded layer of snow) is to the next snow layer underneath. Various mechanisms actually constitute the anchor: simple friction, interlocking crystals, and metamorphic bonding through melting/freezing and sublimation.

When this anchorage is weakened to the point where stress exceeds strength—either by greater weight of new snow, or by metamorphism weakening the underlayer, or by water lubricating the bonding surface—then the slab is considered 'unstable'. It may not fall, however, because it is also anchored on both sides, as well as top and bottom.

The strength of all these anchorages also depends on the profile of the terrain. Remember (especially if the slab has a convex top) that 'creep tension' within the snow is always working to pull the slab away from its top anchorage. The release or triggering of an inherently unstable slab, generally involves 'cutting' or breaking the top anchorage. In any case (whether as cause or effect) a fracture line, cutting perpendicularly into the slope, is always left across the top of a slab avalanche. Now, a closer look.

SOFT SLAB AVALANCHES: These are the most dangerous avalanches for skiers, and the ones most likely to be encountered. We are talking about those slab avalanches that fall *during and just after heavy snowfalls*. The soft slab avalanche breaks away in a slab but doesn't preserve this cohesion—or block-like form—as it slides. It is essentially a soft-snow avalanche that starts from a fracture line, although the snow must have a certain degree of cohesion to begin with.

Soft slabs don't necessarily form in all storms. When do they form? There are many contributory factors. But the principle ones are: density and depth of new snow, the rate at which it was deposited; and also, the action of wind. The more snow and the wetter or denser it is, then the more a given layer or slab will weigh. And the greater will be the force pulling it down the hill. The rate of snowfall is important, because if the snow is coming very fast, much of the normal process of settlement and stabilization is cut short. A high rate of wet or 'heavy' snowfall compounds the tendency to instability. And finally, wind action is important, as it magnifies the other factors—making the snow denser, and aiding the mechanical compaction necessary for new snow to behave like a slab. When most, or all, of the above factors are present (and especially if the old snow surface offers poor adhesion) you should expect a general build-up of soft slab conditions.

Temperature is also important. If the storm begins with wet snow around the freezing point, and later cools to a drier powder, slabs will be less likely. And you may experience only loose powder sloughs (pronounced 'sluffs'). After the storm, the danger will decline as the snow stabilizes and settles on its own. This stabilization, however, will be much faster if the temperature is warm, i.e. around freezing. Extreme cold prevents the plastic deformation necessary for settling, and the soft-slab danger may persist for long periods.

How do you recognize a soft-slab-avalanche condition? Potential avalanches, unfortunately, do not signal their presence with tell-tale visual signs. You must know what produces the condition, and then have a suspicious nature. *Treat all major winter storms as a source of soft slab danger*. Avalanche hazard at American ski resorts is so well controlled, that the downhill skier simply cannot rely on his experience of a few 'powder days' a season in guessing whether snow will slide. Spontaneous sloughs and small soft slab avalanches on steep slopes, although a theoretical sign of stabilization, are a practical warning of immediate danger. Likewise, if you set off small slides or sloughs on easy

safe terrain, you will know that a high hazard exists. Soft
slab formation is general, not limited to certain exposures,
although lee slopes are always suspect.

Terrain can affect both the likelihood of an avalanche,
and its consequences. Gullies are perhaps the worst spots,
for not only are they zones of deposit for wind-drifted slab,
but in a gully the channeled snow of an avalanche will be
deeper, so that less snow can do more damage (or bury you
deeper). Open slopes, and sparsely timbered slopes are high
in potential hazard. Only very densely timbered slopes can
be presumed stable. Wind-battered slopes are *generally* safer
than lee slopes that may have large wind-deposited slabs.
Convex slopes, we've already noted, are the natural fracture
zones, but this doesn't mean that a soft slab can't fracture
elsewhere. And finally, there is the factor of steepness.
Everything else being equal, steep slopes will avalanche
first. (For a given slab, the downhill component of gravity,
or stress, will be larger on a steeper slope.) Any slope
steeper than 30 degrees should be considered suspect in
conditions of general soft-slab formation. But avalanches of
all types can form and release on slopes down to 20 degrees
or less.

HARD SLAB AVALANCHES: These are real traps. In a
sense, they are just a more extreme case of the soft slab
avalanche, with the role of wind (in transporting and compacting snow to form a slab) greatly increased. A hard slab
avalanche tends to slide in distinct chunks or blocks of
compacted snow. Since the slab itself is more dense and
compact, hard-slab danger does not subside rapidly through
normal settlement of the snow. They lie in wait like so
many land mines. There are, however, certain clues.

Hard slabs are generally confined to recognizable lee slopes, and are formed for the most part at low temperatures. Often the only difference between a hard-slab avalanche hazard, and a perfectly safe hard slab of wind-packed snow, is the presence of an unstable snow layer underneath. Depth hoar is the main offender; and the same weather patterns that lead to the formation of depth hoar, also favor the build-up of hard slabs. By and large, touring skiers should seek out and rely on the expertise of snow-safety personnel at ski areas, concerning the possible presence of hard slab avalanche conditions.

When walking or skiing on hard wind-blown surfaces, consider any hollow, drum-like, or rumbling sounds as warnings of an unstable slab. But in the field, the ski mountaineer, or touring skier, will just have to rely on his hunches about hard wind-packed slopes, most of which are probably quite safe. This form of avalanche hazard is more common in the cold dry climate zone of the Central Rockies than further west; and in certain areas hard slabs may constitute the major avalanche hazard.

CLIMAX AVALANCHES: A climax avalanche is a sort of giant slab avalanche, involving a compound slab. That is, the layer that finally slides is made up of a number of layers, none of which were at all unstable by themselves, but which, taken together, finally overcame the supporting strength of some weak layer deep in the snow cover. This weak bond might be a layer of depth hoar, or an old crust lubricated with melt water or rain in spring, or some other unstable strata. Here the touring skier is really over his head. Unless you know the snow history of a region for the entire winter, it is impossible to guess when climax ava-

lanches will occur. Fortunately, they are sufficiently rare
that, statistically, they are not real hazards for the touring
skier. They do appear in cycles, so if an experienced snow
ranger tells you there is serious climax-slide danger in the
area, better cancel your tour.

WET SNOW AVALANCHES: Wet snow avalanches constitute the principle avalanche hazard on a spring tour. And in
warmer, wet climate zones such as the Pacific Northwest,
they can occur year-round. Wet snow avalanches result
from free running water in the snow cover—lubricating
some underlying unstable layer, or lubricating the weak
bond between two layers. They can slide either as loose
snow slides (from a single point), or as wet slabs (from a
fracture line across the slope). Although they move more
slowly than dry snow avalanches, they can do enormous
damage because of the weight and density of wet snow.
(Imagine a slow river of wet plaster-of-paris.)

Rain, soaking the snow cover, is one of the commonest
causes of wet snow avalanches. Another is the 'greenhouse'
effect of cloudy overcast days warming and melting the
snow. Wet snow avalanches are common after heavy spring
snowfalls, especially on south-facing slopes.

There are usually numerous signs of this kind of instability. Rolling 'snowballs' are one; so are small sloughs of
snow beneath one's skis. In high zones, wet-snow avalanche
danger might be acute in the afternoon, although the morning snow was perfect 'corn'. The skier's feeling about the
snow usually gives a clue. When 'spring' snow becomes
'rotten' snow, watch for these slides.

We shouldn't close this section without mentioning cornices again. These overhanging frozen waves of snow, built-

up by wind on the lee side of a ridge, can be as dangerous as they are beautiful. A collapsing cornice is a common trigger for slab avalanches on the slopes beneath.

Practical measures

The best way to avoid being caught in an avalanche is never to leave the packed slope. But once you're hooked on wilderness skiing, that option is no longer open. What you can do about avalanches boils down to the following: Understand a little about them. Get the best snow information available. Learn to recognize unstable snow conditions; and in such conditions, avoid the most dangerous slopes and obvious avalanche paths. If you must cross a danger area, then take a few minimum precautions, and expose only one skier at a time. If you are caught, make vigorous efforts to get out, to stay upright, or at least to remain oriented. If someone else is caught, begin a quick search as fast and efficiently as possible—*never just run off to get help.* Let's cover these points in greater detail.

AVOIDING THE DANGER: The obvious way to find out about possible avalanche danger on a proposed ski tour is to ask an expert. U. S. Forest Service snow rangers, or professional patrolmen responsible for snow safety at major ski areas, will have information that you can only guess at. It's impossible really to assess avalanche potential without knowing something of the general weather pattern in the area. Not only do these snow-safety personnel have the records, and the day-to-day familiarity needed to warn you of any hazard, but they can often suggest slopes or exposures that will add to the pleasure of your tour. They would all rather give you some useful advice than be called to rescue you, or dig you out.

From these professionals, from experienced ski tourers, and with a little judicious research, learn what the typical avalanche hazards are in your favorite areas. In the Sierra, soft slab danger is widespread, but seldom persists very long after storms because of the typically mild weather. In the Northwest, wet snow is the problem. And in the Rockies, extreme cold extends the danger period well beyond actual snowstorms and windstorms. On a more local level, some valleys almost never experience high winds—in other areas, it may be commonplace. Once you've identified some known avalanche slopes, you'll be a lot more confident about recognizing new ones.

The maximum avalanche danger exists during and just after major snowfalls or windstorms. Even in high-risk terrain, the first hours of a storm are probably quite safe. Use them to remove yourself, or your camp, to a safer location. On a long tour, in remote and potentially dangerous terrain, it might be well worth staying put a day or so after a big storm, to let the snow stabilize somewhat. What else can you do?

Become sensitive to the terrain. Learn to spot convex fracture zones at the top of open slopes. Recognize which side of a drift or gully is the lee side, and which the windward. Pick out old avalanche paths where trees have been knocked out from repeated slides. (These large avalanche paths can often be spotted on topographic maps as treeless gullies—indicated in brown ink to show lack of vegetation—descending through slopes of green ink, or forests.)

And then, having learned to spot the dangerous slopes,

make an effort to avoid them whenever conditions seem risky. Theoretically, following a ridge over the top of a dangerous slope is the best procedure; but it's often impossible. You can, instead, often use a series of terrain features —ridges, rock outcrops and densely forested slopes—for temporary 'cover' when moving across a dangerous area.

Become more aware of the snow underfoot. A real 'sense of the snow' is the last thing one learns in skiing—but it is the difference between an average skier and a real master. As snow changes from, say, light powder into a soft slab condition, there are numerous signs which may pass unobserved if you're not already aware of them. The varying surface-texture and resistance of the snow can be felt at each step, or each turn. Your ski may encounter momentary support, which then collapses, dropping you a few inches deeper into the snow—a sign of some sort of slab formation. Cracks in the snow, running ahead and to the side of your skis are even better indications.

Snow-safety personnel frequently use 'test skiing' on a small 'safe' slope to determine avalanche conditions on a large exposed slope. You choose a small slope of the same angle and exposure as the one you're worried about, and try to 'cut' it by traversing, just at the point of maximum drop off (convexity), using heel-thrusting movements with your skis to see if you can set off a mini-slide. This method is far from foolproof because wind exposure on major slopes is almost always different than down below on a safe knoll. It's still a useful procedure, though, and in a sense, an experienced deep-snow skier is 'testing' the snow all the time.

Test skiing, as such, is very useful for detecting soft-slab conditions, but probably won't tell you anything about hard slabs. Certain hard-slab conditions can be recognized by probing the snow (bashing is more like it) with an upside-down ski pole. You can often feel a weak layer, if it's not too deep, or if the slab isn't too hard. Loose snow avalanches of winter powder are rarely more than sloughs, and don't represent nearly the hazard that soft slabs do. In view of the inexorable cement-like quality of dense wet snow, we recommend that you *do not* set off even the smallest wet snow avalanche as a test. Theoretically, it's not impossible to lose one's footing, fall and be completely immobilized under six inches or a foot of wet snow.

IF YOU MUST SKI IT: Eventually, for one reason or another, you'll probably find yourself facing a dangerous slope that you must either cross or descend. What then? In the first place, it's a calculated risk. If you're sure the slope will avalanche, and avalanche big—then don't do it. Even if it means hours of walking back, up, and around by an alternate route. But it's not usually that clear-cut. If you expect only a limited avalanche—small sloughs on small slopes, or a soft slab layer only a few inches thick—then skiing an avalanche path could perhaps be reasonable.

As far as skiing goes, you have two choices. You can traverse the slope at the top, at or above the likely fracture zone—trying to reach a relatively 'safe' spot (further across and further down) by skiing rapidly. All members of the party should follow in the first skiers tracks.

Or, if you must ski the whole slope, then avoid traversing and stay in the fall line, making short turns, as rounded as possible, avoiding edge-set and heel-thrust movements. Traversing, of course, tends to cut the top anchorage of a slab. Ski patrolmen, whose job is to set off avalanches on hazardous slopes, commonly find that a patrolman wedeling down the fall line won't release an obvious slab, which is only brought down by a second patrolman cutting the slope in long zig-zag traverses. Of course our second choice, skiing the fall line, is open only to expert skiers.

Even without soft-slab conditions, the expert skier, linking short turns down the fall line in deep powder, may feel a sort of mini-avalanche or slough following him down the slope. This loose snow (which the skier has disturbed) is not dangerous in itself, although it may cause one to trip and fall. But its weight and movement could trigger a soft slab further down the slope. So it's a good idea to turn out from time to time, and watch what happens to this loose snow as it slides on past.

Weaker skiers are already at a tremendous disadvantage when skiing avalanche terrain (though good skiers are certainly not safe for that reason). A skier's fall might well trigger an unstable slab. And in any case, if you feel awkward on your skis, you won't be able to react decisively should a slide start.

Before crossing a potential avalanche slope, get ready. *Tie on your avalanche cord* if you have one (you should) and spread it out in the snow—it won't help if it's a big tangle. An avalanche cord is nothing more than 50 feet of light nylon line, generally red, and often marked every few meters with a tag pointing to the skier. (This last feature is not essential.) If you are caught in a slide, the light avalanche cord should more-or-less float on the surface; and even if you are buried, there is a great chance that part of the cord will be visible when the slide comes to a stop.

Take your ski-pole straps off your wrist. This is vital. No matter what happens in a slide, you will need both hands free to protect your face, and possibly dig out afterwards.

What about ski bindings and safety straps? A certain controversy exists about whether or not you should take off your Arlberg or runaway straps and loosen your bindings before crossing an avalanche zone. The traditional theory is that the skis will be trapped by moving snow, and can pull you into awkward positions or break your legs, if they don't release instantly. On the other hand, almost all the avalanche-control personnel we know do the opposite. They leave their runaway straps on, and do not loosen their safety bindings; nor do they make a conscious effort to get rid of their skis when caught by a slide. For one thing, there usually isn't enough time. But more important, if caught near the top of a small-to-moderate slide, your skis may be instrumental in helping you get out of the worst of it. Then too, if it's only a small and harmless slide, but has buried your loose skis, you can be in real trouble in the back country. If it's an enormous slide, it probably doesn't matter. It's also a good idea to have your clothing sealed up, i.e. zippers zipped, parka hood up, and so forth, but this is usually the case when one is skiing powder, or skiing in a storm.

Perhaps the most important single thing you can do in a possible avalanche zone is *expose only one skier at a time*. This is a good idea even for skiing deep powder slopes that are presumed safe from avalanches. As one skier crosses or descends the slope, the others watch. And should an avalanche start, their job is *to follow the skier with their eyes and pinpoint the spot where he disappears* (the last-seen spot). This is done not just for the first skier, but for all skiers crossing the slopes, as delayed release of slab avalanches is quite common. Some avalanche authorities have suggested spacing the party out, up to 50 yards apart. But where possible, we would suggest only one man at a time on a dangerous slope.

One nearly foolproof precaution exists—the *Skadi avalanche rescue beacon.* But considerations of price put it out of the range of the average touring skier.

The Skadi is an ingenious solid-state transmitter-receiver, barely eight inches long, which functions as a sort of radio direction-finder. Members of a party equipped with Skadis carry the device in their parkas, turned on (they will run for a week), and switched to transmit. If one skier is buried, the others switch their Skadis to receive and locate the buried victim with a simple search pattern. It's been calculated that a Skadi-equipped searcher looking for a Skadi-equipped victim is the equivalent of nearly 500 men with probing poles. So you can see why the Skadi has been enthusiastically adopted by professional avalanche-control personnel. But, since each unit costs over a hundred dollars, and you need at least two, the Skadi is not likely to become popular with touring skiers. It has been carried, however, on dangerous winter tours in the Alps and in Colorado; and in such maximum hazard areas is probably the only margin of safety. The Skadi is manufactured by *Lawtronics, Inc., 326 Walton Dr., Buffalo, N.Y. 14226.* The firm will send literature on request.

One last clarification. We are *not* suggesting you go out and ski potential avalanche slopes. Every winter at major ski resorts, trained snow-safety personnel ski across hundreds of dangerous slopes, set off dozens of avalanches, and are usually carried away by at least a couple of small ones, and then dug out by their companions. It would be utter folly for the average touring skier to think he could get away with this. For one thing, he is usually skiing on completely unfamiliar slopes that have their own surprises and avalanche patterns. Discretion and prudence are your real defenses against avalanche danger. The skiers who are most exposed are, doubtless, the deep powder enthusiasts. For deep powder skiing is at its best during and just after a storm—when avalanche danger is also highest. Powder skiing is somewhat like driving a sports car at high speeds: the pleasure is so intoxicating, and the consequences of a crash or avalanche so remote and theoretical, that it's hard to hold back. Certainly, the authors have accepted a level of avalanche risk to get some of their best powder runs. But it's vital to know what you're doing, and what you're risking. If you're ever carried down by a small slide, or have the experience of accompanying a professional on his avalanche-control rounds, the theoretical warnings you've just read in this chapter will become more real. *Remember, most avalanche victims triggered the slide that got them.* What did Pogo say? "We have met the enemy, and he is us."

IF YOU ARE CAUGHT: Most slides begin quietly. Even hard slabs produce a dull thump rather than a loud crack. Your first warning will generally be a blurring or movement of the snow surface, or a friend's shout.

If the slide is not big and you are near the top, you have an excellent chance of staying put while the slide passes around you. Dig both poles into the snow on the uphill side (hold them together, and slide one hand low for better leverage), grip the underlying snow as best you can with your edges, and hang on.

If a soft slab avalanche is carrying you slowly downward, try to walk, wade, or ski to the side of the slide. You can only do this with your skis on your feet.

And finally, if a slide starts above you, and you are in a ready-to-ski position, it's worth trying to ski out of the way. Not straight down in an attempt to outrun the slide; but down and to one side to get out of the way. Most of the time this is impossible, but it's better to do something; and in the right circumstances, it might work.

But once you're carried away, what then? It's a good idea to shout to attract your companions' attention. We haven't talked to any experts who believe in the efficacy of the proverbial 'swimming' motions to stay on top; but you must still react. *Make vigorous efforts to stay upright and oriented.* (If you're upright, it will take six feet of snow to bury you; if you're knocked down, one foot may be enough.) Just as you feel the avalanche coming to a stop, you must do the following. *Keep both hands in a protective position near your face and chest. Then, just as you feel yourself stop, cover your mouth with one hand, and reach straight up with the other.* This instinctive gesture of reaching toward the surface has permitted numerous victims to be dug out in minutes; but it only helps if you know which way is up. Likewise, it's vital to protect your face and mouth; not merely to insure a breathing space, but to keep from swallowing cold snow, which may stop your breathing altogether (by possibly inhibiting the vagus nerve in the back of your throat).

As an avalanche comes to a stop, the snow (even light powder) will usually set-up as a hard solid mass. This is due to the sudden release of kinetic energy and to the 'age hardening' of snow during its fall—and it has the gravest consequences for a trapped skier. So in the first seconds, try to make enough room around your face and chest for easy breathing, before the snow hardens.

What now? If the snow permits, try to dig upward. If

you are disoriented, spit or drool saliva onto your lips and face, and feel which direction it runs to determine which way is *down*. But often, digging out is impossible, so you must conserve your energy and wait for rescue. Unless your rescuers are very, very close, don't waste your strength shouting. Snow transmits sound in, but not out; so you will hear them long before they can hear you.

It's easier to say *Don't panic!* than it is to keep calm when you're in mortal danger, but you must make the effort. What if you aren't rescued? Why should your last hour be one of nightmarish fear or exhaustion? Put your thoughts in order, trust in your stars and relax . . . By doing so, you will consume half the oxygen you might otherwise, and your chances of survival will double.

IF A FRIEND IS CAUGHT: The survivors have a lot to do. If the buried victim panics, he will probably pass out; if the survivors panic, their buried friend will probably die. How likely is this?

The time element is critical. It was previously assumed that a victim's chances of being found alive diminished rapidly after two hours. Recent statistics indicate that the time margin is even smaller. After an hour's burial, the victim's chance of being found alive is somewhat less than fifty-fifty. After two hours, it's more like 10 percent. These are only statistical averages, and some of the recorded exceptions are astonishing. People have survived for days, so don't give up after only an hour. But these statistics determine the best tactics to use once someone else has been buried. They tell us that *the hasty search is the most important*. A thorough search, with a reinforced rescue party probing the snow at close intervals, is generally no more than an exercise in body recovery. Let's look at our procedure in detail.

Mark the last-seen point. This is easy to forget, but very important, especially if it is snowing, since new snow may obscure the avalanche traces in a matter of twenty or thirty minutes. The search is narrowed to that portion of the slide directly below the last-seen point.

Make a rapid search. Cover the surface of the slide below the last-seen point, looking for any trace of the victim: poles, gloves, equipment, and especially the avalanche cord (usually of red nylon for visibility).

Examine the terrain. Check for any benches, ledges, or stands of trees that might have stopped the victim, and search for traces in these spots. At this point in the rescue, you are still just kicking and scraping at the surface snow, not probing systematically—except right beneath some found article of equipment or other positive sign.

Begin probing. Use either the heels of your skis, or your ski poles if you can pull the baskets off (as with Scott and other models)—otherwise just use the skis. You must judge whether there are certain likely areas, or whether to probe the whole slide below the last-seen point. Start at the bottom and work up. As many skiers as are available stand in a rough line. You thrust the probe (pole or ski) into the snow in front of you, take one step forward and repeat. Try to probe the full depth of the slide although this will be difficult with skis and poles. How can you tell if your probe has hit a body? You will feel a distinct change of sensation. Or your ski or pole won't go down as far. When the probe encounters a body there is a sudden resistance—different than that of the snow. Bent-over trees which are somewhat yielding to the probe can feel just the same as a body. If you think you've found someone, a few more probes in the same neighborhood will probably either confirm or help reject your suspicion. If there are enough rescuers, most should continue probing the slide while a couple of them dig down to each suspected body location. Don't worry about poking the victim—he will forgive you.

Should you go for help? This is the tricky question. *Never* seek help before making a quick search of the avalanche area. If help, especially an organized ski patrol group, is nearby—for example, if you are powder touring near a ski resort—then send one of your party for help while the rest remain to search, probe and dig. In the back-country, hours or days from help, the question becomes academic. Everyone must participate in the quick inspection of the avalanche, and the rough-probing search that follows. Altogether, more lives have probably been lost than saved by the survivors rushing off to get outside help.

We haven't mentioned it so far, but it should be obvious that if one avalanche has come down, then others are possible. Usually the slope where the victim has been buried is reasonably safe—everything has already come down. But in certain situations, another slide could come down in the same place. It's nonsense to post a so-called avalanche guard to warn you, when all hands are needed for searching, probing and digging. But be conscious of this extra danger, and don't let the searching survivors become victims in their turn.

Looking for a buried skier is a grim business. You must move quickly because of the limited time a victim can survive, and yet stay organized, and search with maximum efficiency. The probable survival time is further reduced by compact wet snow which tends to shut out air and actually crush the victim—or the time may be extended by porous, light, but slightly chunky snow. Statistically, though, it seems as if everything is against a skier who is completely buried by a major slide. Perhaps the best way of tipping the scales back in your favor is to *wear an avalanche cord. They almost always work.*

When you think you've found the victim, he must be dug out. For this use snow shovels (if you have them) and ski tips, which work pretty well. Once you've uncovered the victim, you must give him first aid, warm him up, and generally act in a common-sense way. *First treat for suffocation, by clearing his airway and giving mouth-to-mouth artificial respiration, before you have dug him all the way out.* Then treat for shock and any possible injuries, and get the heck out. (See the next chapter.)

How seriously should the touring skier take this whole subject of avalanches? Reading any chapter or book on the subject, one is apt to get the impression that the winter landscape is a vast white death trap, a no-man's land of unstable slabs, fracture zones and potential avalanche paths. It just isn't so. If there was that much danger, very few people would ever become wilderness skiers and those who did wouldn't last long. Most of the time, in most areas, snow is a friendly medium.

Remember that the forces which produce unstable snow will also stabilize the snow, if given enough time to work. This long-range stabilization means that spring snow is generally safer than winter snow. And so, in high and hazardous ranges like the Alps, most serious ski touring is done in spring, not winter. Spring weather, too, is generally more stable than winter weather.

So, if you can avoid touring during, or just after, big storms, you may well make dozens of trips without ever being exposed to the slightest avalanche danger. The Nordic skier in the East and Midwest may never even see an avalanche slope in the course of a whole season. But, in the Tetons, for example, you may cross them on every tour.

In any case, thinking about avalanches before you get near them is elementary prudence. It's easy to over-dramatize the danger; ridiculous to underestimate it. The ultimate attraction of wilderness skiing is compounded of many mysteries—avalanches are just one such mystery.

8. Self Help In Winter

Self help in winter goes far beyond merely learning the principles of first aid, and occasionally being called on to apply them. It is above all a question of responsibility—of accepting *in advance* the possible consequences of your adventurous inclinations, so that when you find yourself in trouble in some remote location, you can act decisively and calmly.

Just as every skier who loves powder will someday be caught in at least a small avalanche—so every wilderness traveler, climber, trekker or skier, will someday find himself or his companion injured or ailing and a long way from outside help. The role of judgment and preparedness is to *reduce* the likelihood or magnitude of such an accident, not to eliminate the risk altogether. It simply cannot be done.

Let's start by admitting that skiing is dangerous. Even at an organized ski area, with every hazard marked, surrounded by ski patrolmen and with doctors nearby, skiing is still somewhat dangerous. As we head off into the wilderness, the potential danger increases, and the consequences of a small accident become suddenly more serious. The only factor in our favor is that the average wilderness skier is a more self-reliant individual than the average downhill skier.

In this chapter we'll cover some of the worst medical emergencies that might arise on a ski tour, just as we looked at the worst avalanche situations. But we must stress that these extreme problems—frost bite, hypothermia, and pulmonary edema—are generally the result of poor judgment and a lack of awareness of the real dangers, physiological as well as physical, in the winter environment. We will be safer in the long run if we admit that potential danger is actually part of the attraction of any wilderness experience. Rather than ignoring it, let's live with it and prepare ourselves to handle it.

First aid

This is not a first aid text. We recommend studying a good one, in particular *Medicine for Mountaineering* edited by James Wilkerson. We also suggest taking a good first-aid course. The most useful courses are the pre-season Advanced Red Cross First Aid courses, given in conjunction with the National Ski Patrol every autumn in most major cities near ski resorts. These courses are intended to train ski patrolmen; and they put special emphasis on cold-weather problems and such classical ski injuries as broken legs. At the end of the course, the participants undergo a day of practical application at a nearby ski area. There, they get the opportunity to improvise rescue toboggans and take them down the hill with a practice victim. We have only one reservation about these Red Cross first-aid courses—their inherent conservatism. You are generally taught to do only the minimum necessary to get the victim to professional medical help. On a long ski tour in the back country, this is not possible. You are the doctor—and it's always better to do something than nothing. What? The following are some of the basic procedures.

MASSIVE TRAUMA: This simply means that someone's been very badly hurt. A skier who's just fallen over a big cliff, or been buried by a heavy avalanche, would be such a case. There is a standard procedure for these situations, well worth reviewing.

Check the victim's breathing and stop any massive bleeding. You will see at once which is more important. Mouth-to-mouth artificial respiration is the only method worth using, but remember also that once an unconscious victim is breathing, you must maintain an open airway. This is done by tilting the victim's head to one side, after checking that his throat is clear. For if he's lying on his back, head up, he might well choke on his own vomit or phlegm.

Bleeding is, of course, stopped by direct pressure. The usual warnings against tourniquets apply doubly in cold conditions, where the circulation is already impaired. And we will see that maintaining adequate circulation is *the* problem of winter first aid.

Next, treat for shock. At the same time, you will be checking for other injuries or symptoms: breaks, contusions, cuts, signs of concussion and/or internal injury. The treatment of all these latter is more or less standard first aid. But shock needs a few words.

There are different sorts of shock, due to different causes, but all come down to the same thing: A state of general physiological depression, characterized by impaired circulation (insufficient blood pressure and volume). Shock can, of course, be caused by bleeding, external or internal. But it can also be produced by a variety of other causes, including pain and fear. It is particularly serious outdoors in winter, because the shock victim is not producing enough heat, and reduced circulation makes him extremely prone to frostbite and hypothermia.

The treatment is simple. *Rest.* Keep the victim flat, raising the feet somewhat without actually lowering the head. *Warmth.* Use extra clothes, sleeping bags, warm drinks, fires, the body heat of other skiers—and above all, insulate the victim from the snow. *Relieve pain.* Don't hesitate to use morphine for pain. Except, of course, if the victim has a head or serious respiratory injury. If unconscious, he is not feeling pain. Most serious ski tourers have a doctor friend who will prescribe morphine or demerol to be used in such emergencies. (It is ironic that heroin is available on the streets, while the serious mountaineer must often scheme to get necessary medical material for emergencies.) If you don't have morphine, use codeine if available, or aspirin and aspirin compounds. *Reassurance.* Cheer the victim up, tell him he's okay and take his mind off his plight.

It's best to assume that some shock accompanies any major injury, whether or not the victim has the classical symptoms: cold clammy skin, rapid weak pulse, a feeling of weakness and of cold. The need to warm the victim up is so important that it may be best to stop and camp (surround him with goose down, warm bodies and a tent, and provide him with fluids). An accident victim in shock is one step away from frostbite and hypothermia.

PROBLEMS FROM COLD: In winter, cold is always a problem, and staying warm always a challenge. Rather than devote a whole section of the book to the subject of warmth, we have assumed that if the touring skier has adequate insulating and protective clothing in his pack, he will simply put it on when he starts to get cold. Accident statistics indicate that this isn't always so—and that a little basic advice about cold is in order.

How cold you get depends, first of all, on the temperature and the wind. The phenomenon of 'wind chill' is fairly well known today. This wind-chill factor is illustrated in numerous charts, purporting to show that a given temperature plus a given force of wind is equivalent to a much colder temperature. True enough, but all the charts we've looked at vary among themselves as to the actual numerical values, the degrees and miles per hour. Anyway, no one carries a wind-chill chart around with him in the wilderness. Just remember how important wind is in cooling you off. In the right conditions, a strong wind can *more than double* the effective cold you are exposed to.

Equally important is the skier's physical (and mental) condition, and the state of his clothing and insulation. Obviously, an exhausted skier cannot produce heat as well as an untired and physically fit person. Psychological effects are more subtle, for often the mental act of 'giving up' leads to premature and unnecessary exhaustion. It's not uncommon to see two people, dressed the same, in roughly the same physical shape, and exposed to the same cold, react in completely different ways. Invariably, as soon as someone believes he is 'done for,' his bodily functions go into a state of depression. The mechanism is not perfectly clear, but we suspect it entails an insidious form of psychogenic shock. All other things being equal, the stronger and more fit you are, the less you will suffer from the cold.

A skier's clothing can be critical. We've advised against waterproof outer gear at sub-freezing temperature, but if your clothing does get wet, you will be particularly exposed to cold since the 'wicking' action of wet cloth greatly speeds heat loss. Wool clothes are always advised for the mountaineer since they don't have this 'wicking' property, can dry from the inside out, and generally provide a lot of insulation even when wet. We don't think it's necessary to follow this rule of 'wool only'—as wool is often uncomfortable and scratchy—provided you realize the problem and take energetic measures to keep your clothing from getting wet. On a ski tour, wet feet are the most common offenders, and a change of dry socks, which weighs nothing in the rucksack, may make all the difference.

Frostbite, the actual freezing of body tissue, is one of two major medical problems due to cold. Frostbite is caused by reduced circulation in the extremities: hands, toes, feet, nose and ears. Blood circulation is the principal means of heat exchange within the body. Therefore, when the body is no longer able to generate sufficient heat, an automatic mechanism begins restricting the flow of blood in those capillaries furthest from the body's center—thus reserving the flow of blood, and heat, for more vital central organs.

Frostbite begins with slight, then general numbness of the affected part. The skin turns cold and pale white, and eventually black, after which dead tissue begins to separate from living—but this happens days or weeks after frostbite is incurred. The first numbness is not irreversible. Circulation must be impaired for some time before the tissues actually freeze and die. And this is the most important point in the treatment/prevention of frostbite.

In actual practice, most mountaineers and skiers who have been frostbitten have simply neglected to warm themselves up—to restore circulation in the affected parts by massage, friction and the application of heat—before it was too late. *As soon as your feet or hands go numb, do something.* If you don't react immediately, it's all too easy to forget since your feet especially won't feel bad: they just won't feel. On a climb, in an exposed position, the usual thing to do when your feet go numb from the cold is to begin kicking them against the rock. As circulation comes back there will be brief painful tingling sensations, a small price to pay. But the ski tourer, who is generally in more secure circumstances than the alpinist, should sit down, remove his boots, change out of wet socks and rub his feet till the sensation comes back.

Don't be lazy about this. Don't say: 'I'll do it when I get back to camp.' Hands, which move about more than feet and toes, are slightly less susceptible to frostbite. Remember to restore warmth and circulation immediately, at the 'frostnip' stage, and you won't have to deal with frostbite. We've done it many times, and it works.

But should you get a real case of frostbite (persistent numbness for a period of hours, with the skin hard, ice-cold and white) *do not rub or flail the affected part*. At this stage, you will only further traumatize the frozen tissue. The ideal correct treatment is the rapid rewarming of the frozen part by immersion in warm water (around 105 degrees). But once the victim's feet are thawed out, *he must not walk on them*. Evacuate this victim as a litter case. (See next section.) On the other hand, if such evacuation is impossible or dangerous, a frostbite victim can walk or ski a long way on his *unthawed* frozen feet without doing too much further damage.

The problem with all this is that if the situation is so serious that you actually do get frostbite, you will probably be engaged in some sort of struggle for survival—and will be in no position to heat up a large pot of water, thaw your feet out, and then be carried back to civilization. If things aren't really that grim, frankly, there's no excuse for getting frostbite, which can be avoided by constant attention to your hands and feet in extreme cold conditions. (For a definitive study of frostbite, we recommend reading *Frost-*

bite by Bradford Washburn, a monograph reprinted from the 1962 American Alpine Club Journal.)

Hypothermia (from the Greek for 'too little heat') is the other major medical problem due to cold. It is unique in that it isn't necessarily associated with extremely cold temperatures—although in the high mountains it usually is. Hypothermia is a killer. It is the extreme cooling of the body's inner core, and is even more serious than frostbite. We've seen that frostbite is really a defense mechanism the body uses to maintain circulation and heat in the vital core. But this mechanism is effective only up to a point. If the body continues to lose heat faster than it can be produced, then the core temperature will eventually go down. Past a certain point, the process becomes irreversible: the heart begins to 'fibrilate,' or beat in an aimless erratic way, and death follows. Death from hypothermia was formerly called death from exposure, an inaccurate journalistic phrase which doesn't stress the importance of heat loss.

The initial signs and symptoms of hypothermia are: poor coordination, slow and stumbling pace, thickness of speech, intense shivering, muscle tensing, a general feeling of fatigue, deep cold or numbness. The basic treatment is to stop further heat loss by using more clothes and insulation, to help the victim to rest and get his strength back (eating carbohydrates is good), but above all to warm him up—with hot drinks, body heat from others in the party, a fire or whatever. In more advanced cases—the victim's core temperature is now below 90° F.—you will notice a blueness or puffiness of the skin, a decrease in shivering followed by a rigidity of muscles, dilation of the pupils, and a slow, weak or irregular pulse. This patient is in a critical state and must be warmed rapidly. Insulating him is not enough, as his body can no longer produce enough heat. Nor is heating from the outside sufficient, as it is the inner core temperature which is dangerously low. Use hot drinks if the victim is conscious, hot enemas if he is unconscious. Of course, you must also apply external heat such as other bodies in the same sleeping bag, or hot baths if you're near a cabin.

However, it's our conviction that the touring skier must concentrate on avoiding such problems, rather than waiting to treat hypothermia when it occurs. Hypothermia generally affects people in cold-wet-windy situations. And its victims have usually ignored the degree to which wetness and wind accelerate heat loss. Therefore, although serious, we see that hypothermia can be easily avoided. Carry enough protective and insulating gear, and use it. (For detailed documentation, read *Hypothermia: Killer of the Unprepared* by Theodore Lathrop, a small monograph published by the Mazamas.)

There is some danger that traumatic shock from an injury could lead to either frostbite or hypothermia. And indeed, all these conditions—shock, frostbite and hypothermia—are related. They all have to do with impaired circulation and heat loss, whether as cause or effect. To avoid complications of this nature, keep the victim of any winter injury warm and insulated from the snow, and make sure that circulation isn't further impaired by bleeding, tight boots or gear, or by mechanical dislocation as in a fracture.

PROBLEMS OF ALTITUDE: Mountain sickness and pulmonary edema are the main ill effects of altitude. And to date, medical science hasn't fully understood either. Both result from a too rapid ascent to higher altitudes, and the symptoms and suggested treatment are better known than the actual processes that cause them.

Mountain sickness is little more than a general malaise

one gets from going too high, too fast. It may be characterized by lack of appetite, lassitude, shortness of breath after
exertion, nausea and vomiting, insomnia, headaches, or just
plain feeling crummy. Since mountain sickness is not really
a severe illness, the treatment varies from nothing, to taking
aspirins, codeine, or sleeping pills at night, to resting for a
day or two at whatever altitude you start feeling sick.
Going down invariably helps, but this usually means giving
up the tour, so few skiers do this unless they're really
feeling poorly. Mountain sickness occurs commonly around
8,000 feet or higher, and can last for a few hours or a few
days. If you keep climbing, it will probably worsen.

High-altitude pulmonary edema is another story, although it also is caused by going too high, too fast. It is a
serious functional impairment of breathing which, unde-
tected and untreated, has killed a lot of mountaineers at
high altitudes. These deaths were originally blamed on
pneumonia. Like pneumonia, high-altitude pulmonary edema fills the small air sacks in the lungs with fluid, making
breathing progressively more difficult, and leading rapidly
to death at high altitudes.

Pulmonary edema is more of an expeditionary problem
than something we encounter on an average ski tour. But
on ski expeditions to high ranges, it's a very real danger. All
the more so, because the ski-equipped mountaineer can
travel upward much faster than climbers on foot, or on
snowshoes. The speed of his ascent (which short-circuits the
normal slow process of high-altitude acclimatization) makes
the skier more susceptible than other mountaineers to
high-altitude pulmonary edema. A prudent party on a big
mountain should often ascend a little slower than their
maximum pace, or perhaps allow themselves a couple of

extra rest days on the way up. (We are speaking of mountains on the Alaskan scale—not the 14,000-foot peaks of our western ranges, which are usually climbed in a couple of days.)

Pulmonary edema may occur above 12,000 or even above 10,000 feet. The victim experiences shortness of breath (even at rest or while sleeping) and a feeling of pressure in the chest. He coughs, and feels both restless and anxious. Later, he may feel suddenly weak; have a rattling, gurgling, or otherwise noisy and rapid respiration; experience extreme difficulty in breathing; and cough up a frothy blood-tinged sputum from his lungs.

Unless you have medical oxygen (hardly likely), this patient is in big yrouble. The only treatment is to get the victim to lower altitudes fast. A strong *diuretic* (Lasix 40 mg. by injection or the equivalent) may also be given, in an attempt to reduce the free fluid in the victim's system which might be secreted into his lungs—but this is only a temporary measure. You must evacuate the victim to lower altitudes as fast as possible, preferably while he's still strong enough to walk or ski down himself. An altitude change of only a few thousand feet makes an amazing difference.

In any case, don't wait for the worst symptoms to develop: persistent difficulty breathing, even at rest, and any gurgling or wheezing sounds in the chest, are good enough indicators to start back to a lower camp—especially if you're at 14,000 feet or higher. After a couple of days at low altitude the victim is usually well enough to resume the ascent.

Altitude is much more likely to plague the touring skier in the form of intense visible and ultraviolet radiation. *Sunburn* is doubtless the most common medical problem of high touring. Fortunately, *snowblindness* is rare because most skiers aren't foolish enough to take off their dark glasses even on cloudy overcast days. One spare pair of glasses per party might be a good idea for high spring touring. The treatment for snowblindness is darkness: bandage the eyes or use two pairs of goggles to reduce the light. Apply ophthalmic ointment and wet compresses to relieve the characteristic painful itchy sensation.

Sunburn can be avoided with a little thought. Skiers who set out before dawn, often forget to apply sun cream when the sun comes up. Half an hour of unprotected exposure to high-altitude sunshine is too much. On a multi-day trip to a high glacier area, just give up washing your face. Dirt and natural oil will form a fine protective layer.

TYPICAL SKI INJURIES: In earlier chapters on ski techniques, we stressed one basic principle. *Ski with your feet and legs, balance with hands and arms.* Since legs do most of the work, it's not surprising that the most common ski injuries are broken legs—with strains, torn ligaments, sprains and bruises of the legs and ankles next in importance.

Methods for splinting broken legs and taping sprained ankles are well known; splinting is covered with almost compulsive throughness in every first-aid book and course. And you should certainly know all the standard procedures. In this section we'll only comment on a few points especially relevant to ski injuries in the back country.

As we indicated earlier, maintaining adequate circulation in cold weather is truly vital. You must consider this in treating (splinting and evacuating) any skier's fracture. At a ski area, the ski patrol usually splints a broken leg with the boot still on. In the back country (with a possible evacuation time ranging from hours to days) this is the wrong thing to do. Boots are too constricting. Also, by removing the boot, you will be able to verify if there has been any ankle injury—always a likelihood in a big fall, because so much of the stress involved is transmitted through the ankle. If the injured skier has a *fracture-dislocation* of the ankle, then you are facing a vascular emergency. The blood vessels passing through the dislocated ankle will be pinched, and circulation so compromised that the skier will probably lose his foot unless you reduce the dislocation (by pulling outwards, then re-aligning the joint). The same considerations apply to any dislocated fracture, but the ankle is probably the most likely and most critical case on a ski tour.

The same reasoning will rule out traction splints for long evacuations, as they are likely to impair circulation in cold weather. Plastic inflatable air splints are very popular in ski patrol work, and on a big tour you might have one available. These are really excellent; but you must be aware of what a descent or ascent of a few thousand feet will do to the air pressure inside the splint. You'll have to keep it adjusted. (As you go down, the splint loosens up; as you ascend, it will tighten around the broken limb.)

In general, the most neglected possibility for splinting broken limbs—and one of the best—is to splint the injured limb to another part of the body. For example, splint a broken femur to the other leg, or a broken arm to the chest. Statistically, most ski fractures are breaks of the tibia or the fibula, usually not both—so you probably won't face the problems of massive muscle spasm and overriding bone ends.

Outside the realm of first aid, we might well repeat what

we said earlier about ski injuries. The more 'up-tight' you are about getting hurt on skis, the more likely you are to be hurt yourself. Defensive, frightened skiing leads directly to broken bones. Recent studies show that under the influence of sudden fear—as when an already frightened skier loses his balance and falls—muscles can tense to such an extent that (for an instant) the human body becomes a totally rigid, brittle structure, with no elasticity whatsoever. This explains a number of broken legs suffered by frightened beginners on the 'bunny slope' at approximately 0 m.p.h. By the same token, a relaxed experienced skier can come through the most catastrophic cartwheeling falls unscathed. Knowing your limits, accepting them, and staying relaxed about the whole business is your greatest safety factor on a ski tour—as it is at a ski resort and, indeed, almost everywhere.

A lot of minor aches, bruises, and especially blisters can occur on a ski tour. But these really come under the heading of normal first aid. It's pointless to try to duplicate a regular first aid manual in a few pages. We'll leave this subject by once again recommending an Advanced Red Cross First Aid course for any serious wilderness skier. It's a pre-requisite before any ski instructor becomes certified; and it represents the minimum knowledge you need to travel with confidence far from help. (For the contents of a good wilderness first aid and medical kit that has been carried on a lot of remote expeditions, see the first appendix.)

Evacuation

Once a member of your ski-touring party has been hurt,

you have to get him back to the end of the road, civilization, and probably medical care. You don't have many choices about how to do this. Maybe the injured skier can ski out unaided, or with a little help from his friends. If not, you will probably have to improvise a toboggan and haul him out. Occasionally, a ski-touring cabin may be equipped with a proper rescue toboggan, which simplifies things greatly. Or, in certain cases where evacuation is extremely difficult or dangerous, it may be better to camp with the victim and send for reinforcements, or for air evacuation by helicopter. On a day tour, not far from a ski area with organized patrol and rescue service, it's often better to send for help, rather than perform an awkward, fatiguing and possibly hazardous improvised evacuation.

HELPING THE SKIER: Many skiers who are slightly hurt or maybe a little exhausted can complete the tour on their feet, with a little aid. The first thing to do is relieve them of their pack and divide the load among the others. If the skier is somewhat dizzy, say from extreme stomach cramps, it's usually sufficient if another member of the party walks alongside, to prop the sick one up. (Or one helper on each side.)

If the skier is too exhausted to complete the downhill portion of the tour under control, then use a *snowplow carry*. A strong skier is in front, skis spread in a wide braking snowplow. The exhausted skier snowplows up behind the strong one, letting his skis be somewhat braced against the other's, and wrapping his arms around the strong skier's chest. In this position, the skier in front can easily steer, brake and stop for both people; and is effectively supporting much of the weight of the exhausted skier. This is an extremely effective trick that patrolmen and instructors use all the time to get tired, frightened skiers off the hill at sweep time. You should practice it first on an easy slope. (See fig. 28.)

Fig. 28. The Snowplow Carry for an Exhausted Skier

Under certain circumstances, any form of motion on skis may be too much for a weak or injured skier, who might still manage to walk at a slow pace, supporting himself on his poles. Carry the victim's skis and, when necessary, stomp out a path for him in the snow. This is still usually faster than improvising a sled, and speed is often of the essence. We did precisely this on Mt. McKinley to take a pulmonary edema victim down some 4,000 feet in a couple of hours.

IMPROVISING A SLED: It's much harder than you'd

think to make a solid rescue toboggan from a couple of pairs of skis and poles, a few cross-braces, packs and nylon line. But if someone in your party has a little mechanical ingenuity, you'll succeed. All the drawings we've seen of such improvised ski sleds show cross-braces held firmly in place by wing nuts and bolts, passed through cleverly pre-drilled holes in ski tips and tails. But we don't know a single ski-touring enthusiast who has ever drilled such holes in his skis. (For one thing, the skis would probably delaminate as a result of water getting between the layers from these holes.) So we've tried to sketch a practical improvised sled without such gimmicks. (See fig. 29.)

Fig. 29. A Rescue Sled Improvised from One Pair of Skis (two pairs of skis make a more stable sled)

You should make every effort to pad and insulate such a sled. Anyone who's ever ridden in a well-prepared ski patrol sled or Akja knows it's a rough ride at best. Use branches, packs, foam pads and sleeping bags to cushion the sled. Place the victim himself in a sleeping bag, covered with a tarp or tent to keep him from getting soaked by the snow.

Pulling an improvised sled is much worse than pulling a proper rescue sled, which is hell. Either attach ski poles to the sled for pulling; or connect your packs to the sled with nylon line to make a kind of hauling harness. Using more than one pair of skis to make the improvised sled already means that one member of the party will have to walk.

(Though it's possible to make an adequate sled from just one pair of skis.) And in some conditions, it's more practical for the whole party to walk rather than ski. This is especially true on steep terrain, if those handling the sled are not expert skiers—but not on ice, where ski edges always give an extra measure of security.

Two situations are particularly difficult with any kind of toboggan, improvised or fully equipped: long upward traverses, and descending over steep terrain. On a long upward traverse across moderately steep slopes, the sled tends to slip away, and is difficult both to handle and to pull. It's often better to set up some sort of hauling system (if you have a rope) and haul the sled straight up the slope. Then make a horizontal traverse; and thus the problem of guiding the sled is not compounded by that of lifting it.

A rope is almost essential to take a sled safely down steep terrain as well. In addition to the skiers, or walkers, who are handling the sled, a rope should be tied to the rear, and a belay man, responsible for holding it, should ski along behind—safeguarding the sled's descent by passing the rope around trees, or using his skis crosswise to the slope as an extra brake. If you don't have a rope for either of the above maneuvers, you'll just have to be more careful, and work harder.

Where sleds aren't available or are impossible to construct, victims can sometimes be evacuated over the snow by wrapping them in a sleeping bag, then in a waterproof tarp or tent, to form a sort of cocoon, which is pulled over the snow like a sled.

So much for the basics of self help on a ski tour. And in fact, for the whole subject of the possible hazards and dangers in the wilderness skier's environment. After a lot of years spent climbing and skiing in different ranges around the world, the authors have concluded that the most serious hazards and dangers are not in the mountains, but within the party, and in ourselves. Your relation to the winter environment began the day you decided that ski resorts weren't enough. And in that decision are the seeds of all the later skill and knowledge that will make the winter wilderness a playground, not a danger zone.

Sometimes the unbroken white landscape of a ski tour seems like a real mirror. In it we find out about ourselves, and find ourselves—and for this, we love the mountains in winter. Yet no one can love a hostile, dangerous place. The more we love these empty slopes, the more we learn about them. And the more we know about them, the less dangerous they become. As wilderness skiers, too, the more we know about ourselves, the safer we are.

Part III.
The Infinite
Variety of
Wilderness Skiing

9. The Ski-Touring Scene

It would be a herculean—that is to say, impossible—task to describe in one small chapter all the good ski touring areas in North America. Besides, as we've stressed throughout this book, the principal charm of wilderness skiing is that, unlike resort skiing, it cannot be catalogued, or limited by indicating all possible slopes and trails.

But the wilderness skier could certainly use some good information in planning his tours. Mountain climbers and hikers have long had guidebooks to their favorite ranges. Until recently, there have been no such guides for the ski-touring enthusiast. A few handsome, well-researched volumes of this sort have appeared in the last years, each devoted to one particular geographical region. We will mention all of these sources of touring information *en passant*, but they only underscore our dilemma—for an entire volume is scarcely enough to do justice to any single area.

So rather than attempt to write a mini-guide to ski touring areas, we will try in this chapter to capture the flavor, and sketch in the general touring possibilities of the major regions across the U.S. and Canada. A big enough task in itself. We hope our readers will forgive us for beginning with our 'home' mountains: California's Sierra Nevada.

The Sierra Nevada

The Sierra already has such friendly nicknames—the 'Range of Light,' the 'Gentle Wilderness'—and the touring skier will find that they apply just as much in winter and spring as in summer. The Sierra is, in fact, a paradise for ski touring.

Until recently, most touring in the high Sierra was of the Alpine variety. In the last few years, California skiers have rediscovered both Nordic-style skiing and the low Sierra.

The whole Sierra Nevada range is of fault-thrust origin (imagine an enormous slab, tilted and pushed up to the east). And thus, one side of the range, the west, is characterized by gentle gradual slopes; while the other, eastern flank, is formed of steep canyons and abrupt mountain faces. Not surprisingly, therefore, the recent surge of interest in Nordic touring has taken place mostly on the gentle western flank of the range.

Yosemite has become a kind of center for Nordic skiing in California, with a fine touring-oriented ski school, a variety of guided trips and tours, and a vast range of touring possibilities in the rolling country around Tuolumne meadows. There are a few other Nordic ski schools, notably one at Mammoth lakes in the eastern Sierra. And more will doubtless appear in coming years.

North of Yosemite, the Sierra is mostly a region of lower peaks, fairly accessible by road for winter touring. Snow depth here is considerable throughout the winter, even north of Lake Tahoe. In spring, the higher zones further south begin to exert an irresistible attraction on the wilderness skier. And in late March, April and early May, more touring is done in the true High Sierra, from Yosemite south to Mt. Whitney and Mineral King.

Spring skiing, in the steep valleys on the east crest of the Sierra, is a real delight. This terrain is best appreciated on Alpine skis. But due to the generally excellent snow conditions, tours which demand two days in winter are routinely done in one day, or one morning, in the spring. A guide to 28 one-day tours, *Sierra Spring Ski-Touring* by H. J. Burhenne, appeared in 1971. The touring routes described in it are excellent, although they hardly exhaust the possibilities.

There are several long touring routes through the Sierra that have gained a just measure of renown. The entire John Muir trail has been skied several times: a 200-mile epic ski adventure. Less ambitious are trans-Sierra tours from east to west, and vice versa. These generally take about a week. One of the most beautiful itineraries starts at Mt. Whitney on the east, and ends either in Mineral King, or at Lodgepole in Sequoia National Park. An easier and popular trans-Sierra tour goes from Yosemite Valley to Lee Vining on the east side, and is quite suited to Nordic gear, as are many multi-day tours in the northern Sierra. One can also tour for several days between two parallel roads in this area. For example, from the Ebbets Pass road to the Sonora Pass road: or between Highway 40 and Highway 50 in the Tahoe area.

There are even a few touring huts in the Sierra. In the Tahoe area, the Benson Hut, the Bradley Hut and the Peter Grubb Hut form part of a projected series of touring huts, begun but never completed by early Sierra Club ski mountaineers. In Yosemite, the Ostrander Lake Hut is an exquisite old-world structure, in a fantastic setting for intermediate and inexperienced skiers. And in the southern Sierra, the Pear Lake Hut provides a timberline base for fantastic, advanced spring skiing, down endless treeless slopes

When we say the Sierra is a paradise for wilderness skiing, it isn't just chauvinism. We are thinking of the variety of terrain which permits every known style of skiing; of how much of the Sierra has never yet been skied; of the consistent high snow depth, year after year; but above all, of the mild and generally friendly weather pattern. Of course, Sierra storms can be violent; and on the average, they deposit more snow than, say, storms in the Rockies. But the damp (neither dry nor very wet) quality of the snow, abundant sun and mild temperatures, make the Sierra snow cover *more stable* than that of any other major range in the country. Except during storms and in areas of high localized wind, avalanche hazard is usually at a minimum. Even in winter, the Sierra Nevada is still the 'Range of Light.'

But then, perhaps we exaggerate. How can you be objective about mountains you love?

The Pacific Northwest

The Pacific Northwest, land of volcanos and wet snow. Like any generalization, this is both true and false. The maritime climate, and hence the snowfall, is certainly wetter than in any other major mountain region—creating a common wet-snow avalanche hazard, and a real challenge to the wilderness skier's technique. If you learn to handle all the heavy new snow that can be found in the Pacific Northwest, and then go to the Rockies for some true powder skiing, it will seem laughably easy. But as we've pointed out, there is a ski technique for every snow condition; and heavy snow is just another challenge, not an obstacle. But perhaps because of the heavier snow, Alpine skiing seems to predominate in northwestern touring circles.

The image of snow-covered volcanos is inevitable but only tells part of the story. Certainly, the major volcanic summits offer inspiring and ambitious goals for the ski mountaineer; and beautiful day tours are often found around their bases. Mt. Baker, Mt. Hood, Mt. Adams, Mt.

St. Helens, and of course, Mt. Rainier—these volcanic peaks are as much symbols of the northwest as they are wilderness ski slopes. They represent, however, only a franction of the touring possibilities.

This is most clearly seen in *Northwest Ski Trails* by Ted Mueller, a fantastic guidebook to wilderness ski routes in the northwest (although he describes a few resorts too, just for balance). The book is well written, superbly illustrated and modestly priced. It describes 41 ski tours that will make your mouth water. (And most of these tours aren't actually on volcanos.) This book should serve as a model for future ski-touring guidebooks produced for other areas around the country. It is published by the Mountaineers of Seattle, a large club of mountaineers and mountain enthusiasts. The Mountaineers and the Mazamas of Portland, Oregon, are the two leading mountain clubs in the Northwest, and among the most dynamic in the country. And these clubs, through their wide membership, their scheduled group trips, and their ski-mountaineering instruction, are ideal sources of local ski-touring information. As well as being the ideal medium through which to discover new touring companions.

The Pacific Northwest is also the only area south of Canada where roped glacier skiing can be a serious part of your ski tour. And there are still a lot of virtually unskied areas in the Pacific Northwest—in the North Cascades for example—that could offer some very adventurous ski touring indeed.

The Rockies

This is the big one. The Rockies should really be split up into several regions or mountain groups. They form the long central backbone of the United States, and have quite a different feeling and character in Wyoming and northern Colorado than they do in New Mexico. Small adjoining ranges, such as Utah's Wasatch mountains, aren't really part of the Rockies at all, and can differ in terrain, weather and snow conditions. But they all have enough in common that we can describe the general flavor of touring in this vast and diverse region.

Think of the Rockies and you think of powder: light, dry, cold powder. Powder hounds who have skied all around the world say that the Rockies' powder cannot be equalled, and it's true. But this is a source of more trouble than satisfaction to touring skiers. For the same conditions that create such light cold powder also produce extreme avalanche hazard in the wintertime. Thus, while many Rocky-mountain skiers tour away from a resort for a few hours, very few actually go on long extended trips through rugged terrain in midwinter. Curiously enough, in these generally steep mountains, Nordic touring may be the safest in midwinter—since the limitations of the equipment itself will tend to keep skiers on the gentlest, and therefore the safest, terrain. Nordic skiers in the Rockies tend to tour up logging roads, unplowed jeep roads, old railroad beds and so forth.

This generalization, about high winter avalanche danger, is far from absolute. An experienced skier can recognize and take advantage of periods of stability, in the middle of the worst winters, to pull off a great tour in risky terrain. But experience and knowledge are the key. On the other hand, springtime opens up an immense field of perfectly safe Alpine touring possibilities. There are incredible wilderness areas such as the Wind River range in Wyoming, where the touring skier is guaranteed never to see another set of tracks. And the same can be said of a dozen small ranges or mountain groups scattered throughout the Rockies region.

Only recently have Nordic ski schools and guide services been available in the Rockies. But such programs have already proved so successful in the Tetons, at Aspen and Vail and elsewhere, that in a few years it may be possible to learn Nordic ski techniques at any major resort—and then use that resort as a base for one-day tours.

A few such resorts already maintain one or two nearby huts for their touring guests. There are even the beginnings of an organized ski-touring hut system in Colorado, but its development will be slow. Miners' cabins abound in the Rockies, however, and are often used for shelter by touring parties.

The possibilities of first-rate *ski mountaineering*—either skiing to reach a difficult winter climb, or climbing on skis through the more truly Alpine zones—are probably greater in the Rockies than anywhere else in the States. Enterprising Salt Lake City skiers have used skis extensively on the approaches to their recent winter 'first ascents' in the Tetons and elsewhere.

Speaking of 'firsts' and ski-exploits, we should point out that skiers in the Rockies have been doing for some time what we call *extreme skiing*. (See following chapter.) Around Aspen, there's already been some competition to make the first ski descents of steep snow faces in the nearby wilderness. Last year, there was a notable ski descent of a cliff-like face on one of the Maroon Bells. But Bill Briggs' incredible ski descent of the Grand Teton surely tops them all. Naturally, this type of skiing, too, is a spring affair.

The Rocky Mountain Division of the U.S. Ski Association is currently preparing a ski-touring guidebook for Wyoming, Colorado and New Mexico. It will describe numerous tours, and also list ski-guides and touring instructors. This useful book should be ready in 1973.

In terms of downhill-only skiing, the Rockies are already overdeveloped. There are more, and fancier, ski resorts here than anywhere else in the country. But in terms of wilderness ski adventures, the Rockies are still perhaps the least-exploited area in the U.S. A ski traverse along the continental divide (there have been only a couple) is equal to, or even wilder than any *Haute Route* the Alps can offer.

The Midwest

Ski touring in the Midwest? Skiers in California might laugh—but any Nordic specialist knows better. Of course, you don't need mountains to go touring. In fact, the northern and colder areas of the midwest might really be called a 'hot bed' of Nordic touring activity.

The Midwest has an ethnic affinity for Nordic skiing. A large population of Scandinavian and North-European extraction has always been a force in keeping Nordic skiing alive and popular in Minnesota and Michigan. To be sure, in this region, Nordic skiing has often meant ski-jumping rather than ski-running, and this requires a word of explanation. Ski-jumping (which together with cross-country racing makes up the competitive side of Nordic skiing) is a neglected art in our country. For years the only American representatives at international ski-jumping meets came from this part of the Midwest (plus, of course, Lake Placid, New York).

Nordic ski-jumping is not a wilderness sport at all. Practiced on artificially constructed jumps, with heavy specialized skis, it has seemed to us outside the scope of this book.

Nevertheless with its reliance on the skier's own muscles, ski-jumping is still closer to touring than to resort skiing. From this background, with the new availability of cross-country ski gear, a real renaissance of interest in ski touring is now underway in the Midwest.

Much cross-country skiing here, as in parts of the East, is done in prepared tracks. This is not surprising. As man's environment presents him with less challenge, he tends to devise more complicated or more subtle games, to preserve the needed sense of stimulation. Cross-country skiing in a prepared track is just such a game. Not a bad one; indeed a very beautiful one—for the track allows the skier to concentrate on the pure technical challenge of skiing.

Cross-country ski tracks are often maintained by a ski club, and more cross-country ski clubs are being formed each year in this part of the country. Of course, even without a track to ski in, your Nordic ski equipment can give you endless satisfactions on the open snow-covered fields of the Midwest. . . . Day touring, not long trips, is the rule here.

The Central Division of the U.S. Ski Association has published a splendid little pamphlet, the *Ski Touring Handbook*, which describes tours and touring trails in Michigan, Minnesota, Wisconsin, Illinois and Ohio. It also lists clubs and a host of useful addresses, and can be obtained for $1.50 from *USSA Central Division, Ski Touring Committee*, 708 University Ave. S.E. #7, Minneapolis, Minn. 55414.

The East

The thought of wilderness skiing in New England evokes images of Nordic skiers gliding through the stark leafless geometry of lowland forests. But think twice, and you

remember that some of the steepest and most famous
spring skiing in the country (Alpine of course) is found in
New Hampshire, on Mt. Washington's legendary Tucker-
man's Ravine. So, although generally less imposing and less
hazardous in terrain than the West, the East offers an
amazing variety of ski touring.

Still, in winter, most of the good touring is done with
Nordic gear on typically suitable Nordic terrain. More touring is done in up-state New York, New Hampshire and
Vermont, than anywhere else in the East. But other areas,
for example Maine, may well have as many touring possibilities for Nordic skiers.

In non-mountainous areas, cross-country touring goes
hand in hand with cross-country skiing in a track—and this
is as true for the East as for the Midwest. Good tracks for
'pure' cross-country have long been maintained at Lake
Placid and Glen Falls in New York, at Hanover in New
Hampshire, and at Putney in Vermont. And at many other
eastern locations as well.

Good information on eastern touring possibilities can be
had from the *Ski Touring Council*, Troy, Vermont 05868,
and the *Ski Touring Association*, Box 9, West Simsbury,
Connecticut 06092. The Ski Touring Council, in particular,
publishes yearly a small pamphlet-like guide to popular ski
tours in Connecticut, Maine, Massachusetts, New Hampshire, New Jersey, New York, Pennsylvania, and Vermont.
This handy booklet, *Ski Touring Guide*, costs only $1.75.

The East is not, however, an area to be taken lightly—
just because its mountains lack the relief of our western
ones. Bitterly cold, yet damp, weather is the staple of
eastern winter. Touring skiers and resort skiers alike are
obliged to dress much more warmly than skiers in the West

(even though westerners ski bigger peaks at over twice the altitude).

The most truly Alpine setting in the East is surely to be found in the White Mountains of New Hampshire, and also the most bitter weather. Because of record winds and incredible cold, peaks like Mt. Washington are the exclusive winter preserve of ice-climbing alpinists in search of an Eiger-like atmosphere. But in spring, touring in the White Mountains is excellent. The Berkshires, the Catskills, most of the Adirondacks and the mini-mountains of up-state New York are less hostile, and offer splendid Nordic skiing, winter and spring.

Canada

Canada certainly offers far more terrain and a greater variety of wilderness skiing than the States. Since we can't hope to do justice to it in this short space, we'll mention a few areas whose ski-touring potential has particularly impressed us.

In Canada, too, wilderness skiing divides roughly between West and East. Eastern Canadian skiing is characterized by low forested terrain and rolling hills, where steep slopes are the exception. In the West, in Alberta and British Columbia, we encounter a truly rugged landscape: steep slopes, high peaks, glaciers and icefields in a profusion of different ranges. The Canadian Rockies alone are a good deal larger than the entire Alps. And further west, the Interior Ranges, and then the Coast Ranges of British Columbia, provide wilderness terrain of unimaginable richness, complexity, and isolation. This is big country.

Yet despite the possibility of extended expedition-like

ski treks through the remoter regions, much of the Alpine ski touring actually done in western Canada has a semi-civilized almost European flavor. This is because of the numerous mountain huts, many of them constructed by the Canadian Alpine Club. A fine example is the four or five-day ski tour which traverses the Wapta and Waputik ice fields from the Banff-Jasper Highway to the Trans-Canada Highway. After each long day's glacier skiing, you arrive at another hut. This sort of tour isn't currently possible in the U.S.

Nor do we have anything to equal the 'helicopter skiing' offered by Hans Gmoser's guide service in the Bugaboo Cariboo, and Monashee ranges of British Columbia. Using a turbine-powered helicopter to reach a summit or col from which one makes a 4,000-foot powder run—and doing it again and again on peak after peak—may not be the purist's conception of a wilderness ski experience, but it's the powder enthusiast's idea of nirvana. And certainly, it's a far cry from building a cable car to get there, and then decorating the summit with a restaurant complex. The skiing you'll get on one of these helicopter trips is beyond compare. It's also, as you can imagine, very expensive.

Here are some other areas of western Canada, already well-known for their fabulous touring. Garibaldi Park in British Columbia, just north of the popular Whistler Mountain ski resort, offers glacier skiing, ski-mountaineering and long runs with easy access. Little Yoho valley in Yoho National Park, and the Rogers Pass area in Glacier National Park (both also in British Columbia) are known for consistent powder conditions, and offer that rarity, good *winter* touring. The northern Selkirks, and the main chain of the Canadian Rockies, which is accessible from the Banff-Jasper

Highway, offer nearly infinite possibilities to the ski mountaineer—but they are generally visited in spring (late March
or April). In fact, April is perhaps the ideal month for
planning any really serious ski mountaineering or 'high
touring' venture. The weather is almost always moderately
stable, and the snow cover more-or-less consolidated by this
time of year.

Finally, in addition to the Wapta-Waputik icefields traverse, mentioned above, a splendid tour traverses the Mum-
mery and Freshfield icefields along the Great Divide. These
icefield tours are some of the finest in Canada. Not so much
because of the skiing, which is good, but because of the
truly surrealistic nature of the landscape. These are not
back-yard mountains. They seem, to the touring skier
dwarfed in the midst of so much solitude, like endless white
oceans, frozen within some infinite time-warp outside the
twentieth century.

Alaska

Alaska is still, despite Yankee dollars and oil companies, a
wilderness state. With so much wilderness, it's hardly surprising that there are so many possibilities for wilderness
skiing, and that so few skiers have taken advantage of them.
This is due more to the vastness of the country than to any
lack of enthusiasm on the part of Alaska's small but growing ski population. For touring and resort skiing both
started at about the same time in Alaska. So the touring
ideal was accepted there before the commercial pressures
for resort development could lay exclusive claim to the
public's winter imagination—as was the case in the lower
forty-eight states.

All styles of touring are appropriate in Alaska. In two major cities, Fairbanks and Anchorage, Nordic clubs and groups maintain fine cross-country tracks. Heading into the Alaskan back country, we find that modified Nordic equipment (heavy boots, cable bindings, etc.) is very popular both with skiers traversing wilderness ranges, and with mountaineers approaching remote peaks. For major ski descents of big peaks at higher altitudes, traditional Alpine ski gear is preferred. Mt. McKinley, for instance, has been skied several times now.

If Alaska is a big and wild place, there is still one compensation—there aren't many people yet, and they are universally friendly. So it should be easy to get ski-touring information from local touring people in Anchorage or Fairbanks about any projected ski trip.

The one time we were in Alaska for a big ski trip, we got the warmest reception we'd ever had from a group of mountain enthusiasts in Anchorage we didn't even know. And we suspect it would be the same for anybody. The wilderness skier, like the mountaineer, belongs to a very special fraternity of people, a community that doesn't recognize regions or borders.

10. Beyond Touring

Is there anything beyond touring? Not necessarily. Certainly, wilderness skiing is an end in itself. In its esthetic and emotional aspects, in all it offers as sport, adventure, recreation, and discovery of self and nature—ski touring is self-sufficient and complete. But there is one sense in which we can go beyond touring.

Even if we begin as backyard Nordic skiers in a local park, ski touring usually leads us into the mountains. Our skis enable us to relate to mountains in winter in a way that is incomprehensible to the summer foot traveler. When the snow flies, the hiker is trapped: we are set free. But even the most experienced wilderness skier is not completely free in the winter mountains. There are places he can't go, for his skis themselves have limits.

The limits of ski touring are those of steepness. But how steep is steep? The average skier, even if he is an experienced mountaineer, will make the most outrageously inaccurate guesses about the steepness of his favorite slopes. Measured in degrees, a slope is always less steep than it looks. Especially when viewed from above—and this is the perspective a skier usually retains.

For the skier, slopes under 10 degrees are quite easy: real beginners' hills. Slopes from 10 to 20 degrees are considered moderate intermediate slopes, quite respectably inclined. Steep slopes (believe it or not) are those ranging only from 20 to 30 degrees. This doesn't sound like much, but it's certainly enough to frighten weaker skiers. Slopes from 30 to 40 degrees are dramatically steep for skiing: the exclusive province of real experts. And even the expert may feel uncomfortable and insecure here, if conditions aren't just right. Somewhere above 40 degrees, skiing gives way to mountaineering.

Of course, with enough technique, training and guts, you can keep your skis on a while longer in this transition zone. In recent years, expert skiers—of whom the most famous is the Swiss guide, Sylvain Saudan—have realized some astonishing exploits on skis. In Alpine circles a subtle competition has developed around making the 'first ski descent' of slopes, couloirs and mountain faces, hitherto considered impossible to ski. These skiers have certainly skied slopes over 45 degrees. And steeper than 50 degrees has been claimed, though we are extremely skeptical. At this angle, the experienced alpinist is clinging to the slope with ice axe and hammer, and moving up on the front points of his crampons.

Needless to say, such *extreme skiing* demands the finest Alpine ski equipment, an expert's technique, and perfect snow conditions. It is not stunt skiing, but a legitimate ski adventure. And we ourselves admit having succumbed more than once to the lure of frighteningly steep, unskied slopes.

In this chapter we will cover special techniques for extreme skiing. But also, and more important for the average touring skier, we will introduce the basic techniques for high-mountain travel and roped climbing. When the mountains get too steep, most of us, most of the time, take off our skis and put on the rope. Without becoming an expert mountaineer or alpinist, learning basic climbing and roped safety techniques should extend the full range of your winter freedom. From the road-head, up through the low valleys into the high cirques, and eventually to the summits —it will be *your* winter wilderness.

Extreme skiing

It's a matter of open debate whether or not there is a special separate Alpine ski technique for very steep slopes. But as slopes approach the upper limits of steepness, most top skiers do have one particular approach to turning. They link acrobatic jumped turns down the fall line, pivoting their skis very rapidly, *in the air*, from one horizontal edge set to another. While on the snow, the skis are kept as horizontal as possible for braking. The track is a stair-like series of interrupted sideslips. The skier suppresses all tendency to 'carve' an arc or slide forward on the snow, and thus his only progress is a staccato downward motion. This motion is brought to an almost complete halt with each edge-set—thereby keeping the skier under control.

Before looking at the extreme turn itself, what about the crucial *edge-set*? This merely means digging one's edges suddenly into the slope—with an inward push of the knees and ankles, and a downward settling of the whole body. Why? In order to stop downward momentum, and feel a solid 'platform' underfoot, from which to spring off into the coming turn. Just before you set your edges, you are actually sideslipping in an *anticipated* position (bust pivoted toward the valley). Attentive readers and advanced skiers will recognize this as a form of the *counter turn* we discussed under advanced Alpine techniques in chapter 3. By the way, edge-sets are very useful in skiing hard-packed slopes, and have many more forms than the one we describe here.

THE TURN: The whole turn for steep slopes is quite

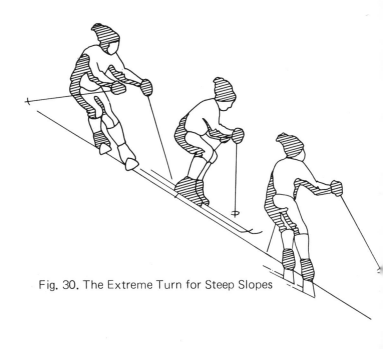

Fig. 30. The Extreme Turn for Steep Slopes

complex. Although it is executed rapidly, we will describe it in slow motion. To follow it in detail, see figure 30. The extreme turn has four phases: a preparatory sideslip, an edge-set which stops the skier and launches the next phase, a simultaneous leap and pivoting of the skis, and finally, a landing with the skis already facing the opposite direction —which leads to the next sideslip and the next turn.

Now to start. Get ready to turn with a *short sideslip*,

almost straight down: body anticipated, your downhill
hand reaching down below your boots with the pole, and

your weight on your heels. (Weighting your heels facilitates the edge-set, and keeps you from sideslipping forward.)

Next, set your edges to stop your motion down the hill, plant your pole and, supporting yourself on it, *immediately spring straight up.* You will not straighten your legs though, but keep them bent, just as they were when you stopped with your edges. In effect, this tends to raise the tails of the skis off the slope and bring the skis into a downslant, more in line with the true angle of the slope. You can see that just trying to turn the skis in a horizontal plane would make the tails bump into the slope itself.

Along with this upward spring or rebound—mostly it isn't a real rebound, as you're going so slow—*you quickly and energetically pivot the skis 180 degrees in the air* till they point across the hill in the opposite direction. In this way, the initiation or launching phase really includes the whole middle or fall-line phase of the turn as well. By thus eliminating the usual rounded follow-through of a parallel turn, the skier can then, upon landing, go into another short skid and set his edges once more. At this maximum steepness, any direct sliding on the snow would quickly accelerate the skier past the point of no control. But, before explaining this end phase of our extreme turn, let's take a closer look at the rapid initial pivoting of our skis.

In the first place, you will automatically be in a wide-track position. (On extremely steep slopes, the uphill foot is naturally much higher, and thus further away from the lower one.) You use this wide stance, plus your continually bent knees, to add power to the pivoting effort. As you pivot your skis, feel yourself in an almost semi-seated position: your knees well in front of your hips, and the tails of your skis somewhat tucked up under you to keep them from hitting the snow behind your back. Remember, you are facing downhill, or anticipating, all the time. In this turn, you are actually pivoting the skis directly underfoot. But you can do this best, if you *concentrate on lifting and moving your ski tips in front of you*.

What then? From an edge-set, you have successfully leaped up, and rapidly pivoted your skis in the air to face the other way—although you yourself continue to face downhill. Now, the landing. Once again, try to conserve the wide stance. If you land with feet together, the slightest crust or drift on the surface will topple you over downhill, an unpleasant prospect indeed on slopes of this angle. Whereas in a wide stance, if either ski 'catches its edge' on the landing, you can still support yourself on the other ski—while using your poles to regain balance. As your skis again make contact with the snow, absorb any shock with relaxed legs—and immediately sideslip into a new edge-set, from which you will repeat the turn back to the other side. You will want to avoid any forward or across-the-hill motion, especially if you are skiing in cramped surroundings, such as a narrow couloir with rocks on both sides. To make sure that you only sideslip vertically downward after landing, *you must land with your weight on your heels*. (Weight on the balls of the feet will initiate a forward carving of the skis.)

The final pattern, therefore, is: sideslip, edge-set, leap-and-pivot; sideslip to a new edge-set (skis pointed the opposite way), leap-and-pivot again; sideslip once more, and so forth, the anticipated bust, facing always downhill.

If you think this turn sounds complicated and difficult, you're right: it is. This is a form of super-stable, super-safe *short swing* or *check wedel*—in which the *horizontal edge-*

set that ends one turn (and serves as launching platform for the next) brings the skier to a virtual stop. It has been called a 'windshield wiper' turn because of the side-to-side displacement of the skis. But actually, this is not a new turn. It's just an extreme variation of our old familiar advanced parallel turn from a counter turn. And this gives us a few hints on how to use it.

The turn we've just described is an extreme one. It is appropriate on the steepest slopes where a fall might be disastrous and where the skier finds himself at the very limits of his technical ability to turn. Of course, the slope may be a shade less steep, or the skier himself a veritable genius—so that actually, a variety of such turns is possible. If things are going well, you can substitute an actual rebound for the muscular leap upwards, or even keep the skis on the snow throughout the turn. (Although you still want a rapid start and a rapid finish, and almost no middle phase.) But if the slope is in the range we call 'desperately steep', even the strongest couloir-specialist will probably jump his first few turns.

How do you learn this *maximum check wedel* or *extreme short swing*? By first mastering classical short swing on moderately steep and hard-packed slopes, and then seeking out progressively steeper slopes—at first in small doses. Why hard-packed slopes? Doesn't this turn work in steep powder too? Powder slopes *can* get awfully steep. But it's our contention that skiing *maximum* slopes is only possible on consolidated or spring-type snow. At 40 degrees, a powder slope will almost certainly avalanche or slough off as you ski it. And if you're not carried away, you will still wind up skiing on the harder snow exposed by the slough. The ideal surface for steep couloir skiing, and other such exploits, is frozen spring snow, warmed just enough by the sun so that a strong edge set (completely stopping your momentum) is easy to make. At the top of such a slope, try a couple of heel-thrusts and edge-sets. If the snow is too hard for a good edge-set, don't even try the first turn. Daredevil techniques will not get you down such slopes. Nonetheless, it often takes a real gut effort to find the courage to launch the first turn.

A few more warnings for slopes of maximum steepness. Above all, don't get nervous and try an exaggerated stem christie (by tilting your top ski almost to the fall line and then stepping onto it). This turn works all right, but gives the skier a lot of forward momentum as he comes out of the fall line. That would be a disaster in a narrow couloir. Also be wary of poles with solid, fairly rigid plastic baskets. These baskets, which are ideal for general touring and for powder, tend to glance off a steep hard surface. If you're counting on the pole for support (as you always do on a steep slope), this nasty surprise could cause a fall. Anyway, you get nervous waiting for it to happen. The best baskets for steep hard surfaces are the Scott type, a thin rubber triangle in the middle of a metal ring, that will give and adapt itself to the slope.

JUST IN CASE: But what if you get on a slope, and only then find it's too steep to turn? You must do something. So try a *ski glissade*. This is a sideslip, braced against one's poles. Start by taking your ski-pole straps off, and use the two poles together as a kind of brace or third leg. You hold them together (uphill hand near the baskets, the other hand near the handles) both poles reaching diagonally across your body to the snow. You can actually support some

weight on them and stabilize your position. By bearing
down with the uphill hand, the scraping action of the pole
tips will reinforce the braking effect of your sideslipping
skis. Practice this once before you need to use it. (See fig.
31.)

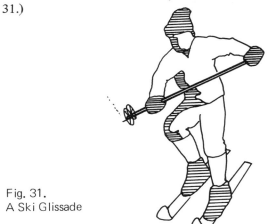

Fig. 31.
A Ski Glissade

Yet one day you will fall. You have already fallen
hundreds and hundreds of times, learning to ski, and becoming an advanced skier or expert. Most of these falls
weren't so dangerous. But what about a fall on the sort of
extremely steep slope we've been talking about? Or on a
less steep but icy slope, which is just as bad. The best
solution for stopping a fall in these extreme, and extremely
dangerous situations, is the *skier's self arrest*.

You can't do a self arrest with your ski-pole straps on
your wrists. So we always remove ours in a situation where

Fig. 32
A Skier's Self Arrest

a fall could have dramatic consequences: cliff bands below, icy slopes dead-ending in rocks or obstacles, and the ultra-steep couloirs and faces we like to ski in the spring. If you fall, your first reaction should be to 'hit' your edges—a sort of 'sitting edge-set'—and bounce back to your feet, with a push of the uphill hand against the snow. But if you can't do this, if you've fallen head-down for example, or lost a ski, then use the self arrest.

Drop one pole. Grip the other with both hands quite close to the basket. Try to get onto your stomach, and *slowly dig the point of the pole into the snow or ice.* You must keep your arms bent, and the point of the pole more-or-less directly under your face or upper chest where you can lean on it with all your weight. It's important to grip the pole close to the basket in order to 'lever' it effectively into the snow. Nor will you stop right away. It may take 50 to 100 feet—but it's better to stop slowly, than to have the pole ripped out of your hand. And it does work. This will stop your fall where nothing else will. (See fig. 32.)

We should also mention that the worst falls on such steep slopes result from losing one's skis. Therefore, under no circumstances should you ski extremely steep or icy terrain with loosely set safety bindings. If anything, tighten them up. For this type of extreme skiing, you need a binding with high elasticity—one you can trust not to release from the sudden shock of a brutal edge set, or a momentary impact. At the moment of writing, the Nevada II and Salomon 505 toe pieces are the only ones we trust completely in this respect. Bindings are improved each year, however, so this will change.

Are there any special skis for such extreme Alpine skiing? Not really. We recommend a slightly shorter than normal ski. Sylvain Saudan, perhaps the greatest specialist of this art, uses normal-length 210 cm. skis; yet other European 'extreme skiers' have used skis 180 cm., or shorter. So take your choice. High, stiff, plastic downhill ski boots would definitely be preferred for this kind of skiing —since control on such slopes is much more than a question of style. It's often a question of survival.

Roped skiing & crevasse rescue

Occasionally, ropes have been used to protect the sort of extreme ski descents described above. But most of the time, a touring skier will only put on the rope to protect himself in a zone of dangerous crevasses—that is, numerous crevasses, or else thinly bridged ones. At this point, the skier has already crossed over into mountaineering.

Here, we shall outline the basic procedure for roped travel on skis. But remember, the more climbing experience and instruction you can get, the safer you'll be when you finally have to rely on the rope. (Climbing knowledge is even harder to transmit in written form than is ski technique.)

Ideally, a roped party in a crevassed glacier area should consist of three or four skiers. But you may have to rope up with only two. In that case, divide the rope in thirds. Have each man tie on one-third of the way in from his end. The rope between the two skiers thus is only one-third the total; and each skier carries his spare one-third around his shoulder in coils. This spare end can later be lowered into the crevasse as an aid in extricating the other skier who has fallen in. A three-man or four-man party will tie in at both ends and in the center.

To tie in to the climbing rope, you can use either a bowline (for the end of the rope) or a simple overhand knot (for tying onto the middle of the rope). Since you may be obliged to hang from your waist for a few minutes, it's a better idea to tie the rope to a *swami belt*. This is a piece of one-inch nylon webbing, wrapped a few times around the waist, and secured with a ring bend or simple square knot. The climbing rope is then tied directly to the protective

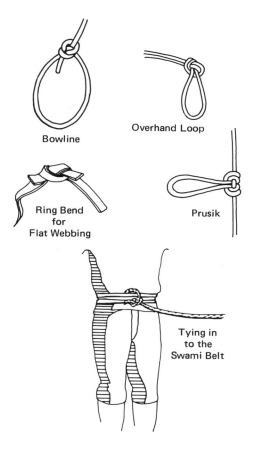

Bowline

Overhand Loop

Ring Bend
for
Flat Webbing

Prusik

Tying in
to the
Swami Belt

Fig. 33. Knots for Roping Up

girdle of the swami belt with a bowline. We've mentioned a lot of knots in this paragraph: most are easy to tie. (Study them in fig. 33.)

You will need to master one more knot: the *prusik knot* (fig. 33). The prusik knot is the key to getting out of a crevasse, and a number of other ticklish situations as well. The prusik knot, as you can see, is tied with a small cord (of 5 to 7 mm nylon rope, not flat webbing) around a full-size rope. It will *slide freely* up the main rope when there's no weight on it; but with weight applied, *grips fast* and remains in place. Obviously, slings or loops of rope, tied to a climbing rope with prusik knots, can serve as movable stirrups with which a climber can ascend the rope. He stands in one loop and slides the other one up. Then he stands up in that one, and repeats the process. For security a third loop, also tied with a *prusik* to the main rope, is added to the system. This third loop passes around the skiers chest and under his arms, as a kind of 'safety.' Now, he has three prusik knots to move alternately up the rope. *Prusiking* is the simplest and most effective, and often the only, way for a climber to ascend a rope. The basic set-up for prusiking is shown in figure 34. If only two slings are available, they can be tucked through the climber's waist-loop or *swami belt*, which then serves as a sort of 'safety,' preventing him from falling backward. Also, instead of one long prusik sling, many climbers use small loops, just to form the prusik knot. And then they clip long stirrup-like slings of flat webbing (used in 'artificial climbing') to these prusik knots with a snap link or carabiner.

But how does this relate to the skier? Prusiking is not

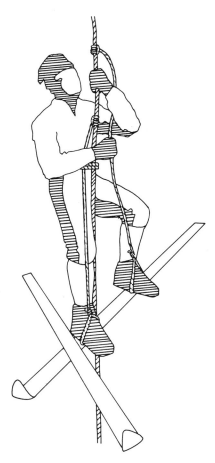

Fig. 34. Prusiking Up a Rope

in. Other methods use pulleys, for mechanical advantage, or a second rope from above. These are interesting, and in certain circumstances very efficient ways of getting out of a crevasse. Skiers who plan to do a lot of glacier touring, should read about these methods in specialized mountain-eering texts, and then practice and master them. Especially the so-called Bilgeri method, involving an extra rope from the surface. But here we are covering only the prusik method. We consider it the most important, because the fallen skier or climber can rescue himself without assistance from the surface—although such assistance is always appre-ciated, and usually speeds things up tremendously. Now that we're roped and ready (and we know how to prusik) let's see what happens step by step.

Roped skiing itself is simple, although it is frustrating, slow and awkward. You can forget about graceful turns if you're skiing downhill, and resign yourself to snowplowing quite slowly, to avoid tangling your ski tips with the rope. On a roped descent, the first skier goes at a snail's pace, and those behind him try to maintain the same slow speed, so that the rope is more-or-less tight all the time.

Each skier has already tied his prusik slings onto the rope just in front of his waist, and carries the loose ends over his shoulder or in a pocket. Middle-men should have at least one prusik sling on the rope in front, and one behind, as they don't know which rope they will be hanging from in case of a fall. You should also have thought about how you will take your skis off, if you find yourself hanging at the end of the rope. Most bindings can be removed by flipping some lever, generally with the basket of a ski pole; and if your Arlberg runaway straps are fastened, the skis will then dangle from your ankles, while your feet are free to be put in the prusik slings. But we're getting ahead of ourselves.

As soon as one member of the party breaks through a snowbridge and falls into a crevasse, the others should drop to the snow, *pivoting both skis crosswise to the rope*, and digging their edges into the snow to resist the pull of the fall. Obviously, you brace your skis between you and the crevasse; that is, your body is on the snow behind the dug-in skis. This stops the fall. In addition, the rope will probably bite into the lip of the crevasse, creating friction which helps you stop the fall.

The next step is for the skier or skiers on the surface to anchor the rope solidly. This can be tricky, especially if there's only one skier. In that case, it's best to use a loop already tied in the climbing rope, through which the skier who has held the fall can stick his ice axe into the snow (after taking it off his pack). If there are two skiers on top, the one furthest from the crevasse anchors the rope to an ice axe or a ski driven into the snow, while the other supports the fallen skier. Once the rope is anchored, shout to the fallen skier that he can begin his ascent.

Here, we've assumed that someone has fallen in pretty far. But if you were all skiing with a tight rope, the trapped skier may only be a few feet in, or still half visible. He will only need a little help over the edge, and won't have to make a complete prusik ascent.

But in the worst case—suppose you're twenty or thirty feet down, maybe not even touching the walls—you will have to prusik up to the surface. You must take the following steps. Immediately, get your skis off and let them dangle, while you get your feet into your prusik slings, sliding at least one sling up, so you can take your weight off your waist. The next step is to arrange the chest sling so you can lean back in it and free both hands. (Or, a fallen man may want to sit in this third sling a moment, while he gets organized.) If you are wearing a big pack, you must take it off, and attach it to the rope (either with a knot, a carabiner, or yet another prusik sling). Or, if a rope is available from above—for example, the other third, or 'tail,' carried by your partner—you can tie your pack and skis on, and have them hauled to the surface. In any case, you are now ready to begin your ascent.

You prusik slowly to the surface. Save your strength to struggle with the lip of the crevasse, where the rope has invariably dug in—making the last few feet, or yards, difficult if not impossible to prusik in the normal way. Once again, if another rope is available, you should tie on and be 'belayed' from above. Or possibly, as you near the surface, you can transfer your prusik knots to the second rope—under which a ski, pole, or axe has been passed to keep it from likewise digging into the lip. If there is absolutely no help from above, and you have an ice axe, you should attempt to cut the rope free from its groove, to cut away the lip itself, or to cut holds in it, so that you can climb as well as prusik. There is no easy answer to this one. Except that, by the time you have prusiked to the surface, you will have a big loop of slack hanging from your waist; so you may be able to unrope and throw this slack to the top man, even if he has no slack to throw you.

Generally, it will take a little help from your friends to get you out. Although if your prusik knots are ready to go, you can probably escape on your own. It's no use, however, trying to figure all this out, once you're hanging inside a crevasse. *You must practice prusiking beforehand, if you expect to use it in crevasse rescue.* You can practice this in your backyard, by prusiking up to a tree branch, twenty or thirty feet off the ground.

How likely are you to fall into a crevasse? Not very likely, especially if you are a good routefinder, and have a nose for where the hidden crevasses are hidden. You can either cross crevasses very gingerly: shuffling along, with one ski way ahead of the other, to spread the load out on the snow bridge; or else, take a couple of skating steps and push off with your poles, to glide across the snow bridge, which also decreases the loading. In chapter 5, we described skiing safely through an icefall area, where other parties had already broken through into crevasses. But we were roped up, and we had thought about what we would do if someone fell in. In fact, we were each carrying Jümars, mechanical handled clamps made in Switzerland, which work like prusik knots but a little better. They are expensive and weigh almost a pound. Nonetheless, if you're skiing over dangerous areas, honeycombed with crevasses, using Jümar ascenders (or similar brands) might save a lot of time and grief.

Basic climbing skills

If, on reading this book, it's occurred to you that skiing is a complex multi-faceted activity, then we should warn you that climbing and mountaineering techniques are even more varied, even more complex. But there is a little bit of un-evolved ape in all of us. Given a broken rocky face, children will swarm right up it without a second thought—even if grownups tend to be more up-tight, and concerned about the possible consequences of a sudden slip.

Rock climbing techniques of great subtlety have been

developed. And for the clearest exposition of the crags-
man's art to date, we recommend you read *Basic Rockcraft*
by Royal Robbins—a real gem of a book. For comprehensive treatment of mountaineering techniques in general
(snow and ice as well as rock), we suggest any or all of the
following: *Mountaineering* by Alan Blackshaw (a Penguin
paperback), *On Ice and Snow and Rock* by Gaston Rebuffat, and *Mountaineering: Freedom of the Hills* by the
Seattle Mountaineers. Each of these volumes has its good
points and its weaknesses. None has satisfied us completely,
but are all interesting.

We will rely on the reader's more-or-less instinctive ability to climb on rock. And we will concentrate on explaining
the basics of snow-and-ice technique, where progress depends on the use of special tools: ice axe and crampons.
And finally, we will say a little more about using the rope
for 'belaying', or safeguarding, the climber's progress. What
follows is not really a how-to-do-it text, but some information that should help you make the transition from mountain skiing to mountaineering.

TECHNIQUE FOR CLIMBING: The snow-and-ice climber's
basic tools are his *ice axe* and his *crampons*. The ice axe has
been the classical symbol of mountaineering for ages. Crampons, more esoteric, are spiked metal frames strapped to
the climber's boots to give him purchase on hard snow or
ice. Modern crampons have twelve points, ten sticking
straight down all around the foot, and two projecting
forward in front of the toes.

For most slopes, the essence of crampon technique consists of placing your feet *flat against the slope*, so that all
ten bottom points can bite into the snow or ice. One tends

to walk upward, with the feet pointing sideways like the
skier side-stepping up a slope (except that instead of 'edging' as with skis, you must roll your ankles *out*, to flatten
the crampons against the slope). On really steep slopes, the
climber simply kicks his toes straight into the slope, and
moves up on his 'front points.' (Sometimes, the first four
points will actually be gripping.) In practice, there are
numerous subtle variations, and skillful cramponing demands a lot of practice; but in theory it's quite simple. A
skilled alpinist can crampon up near-vertical slopes, using
axe or ice hammers for balance. But when things get too
scary for the average climber to trust his crampon points,
barely penetrating the surface, he must resort to cutting
steps with his ice axe.

The ice axe is more of an all-purpose tool than are
crampons. Mountaineers frequently use their ice axe as a
cane, long before it is technically required to climb with.
We frown on this practice—for one thing it encourages
people to buy ice axes too long for serious climbing, 70 to
80 cm. being the proper length. And we suggest that if a ski
mountaineer needs a cane or prop (very handy at high
altitudes, or in deep snow), he should use both his ski poles,
and keep his ice axe in the pack. German and Austrian
climbers were the first to make extensive use of ski poles on
big snow climbs, even when they didn't take skis. The
practice should be more widespread (though we're not
talking about steep slopes).

The ice axe, however, is still the climber's most important tool in snow-and-ice climbing. For even if you don't
have crampons, you can always cut steps with your axe and
keep going. But at first, the ice axe is used as a handhold.
As the slope steepens, you jab it into the snow above you,

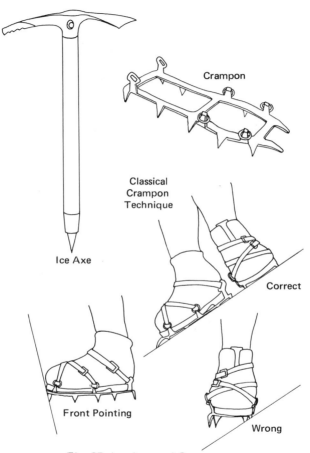

Crampon

Classical
Crampon
Technique

Correct

Ice Axe

Front Pointing

Wrong

Fig. 35. Ice Axe and Crampons

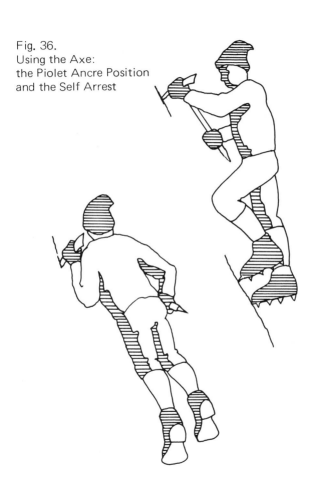

Fig. 36.
Using the Axe:
the Piolet Ancre Position
and the Self Arrest

and always hold onto it, as a sort of self-belay while you move up. On traverses, the axe is held in the uphill hand. While ascending directly up moderately steep slopes, you often grip the axe-head with both hands, like a handle, as you thrust the shaft into the snow. The security you get from a well-planted ice axe is considerable. If the snow is not too hard, you can often kick steps up a slope, without crampons, using the ice axe for balance.

On steeper, harder snow or ice, the ice axe and crampons are used together as part of a more sophisticated technique. The key here is to hold the ice axe in the position of *piolet ancre*, that is, one hand on the axe head and one on the shaft. In this position, you can plant the pick of the axe above you, and use the axe for support as you crampon a couple of steps higher. (See fig. 36.)

This same position, *piolet ancre*, is used to make a *self arrest*. More effective than the ski-pole arrest described earlier, this maneuver will stop you if you fall on soft or hard snow, and even on easy low-angle ice. On hard steep ice you must rely on the rope, or better yet, don't fall. To do a self arrest, the fallen climber who is sliding down the slope, must get on his stomach, his head pointing uphill, and *slowly grind the pick of the ice axe into the snow*. The axe is held across the chest, top hand on the axe-head, other hand gripping the shaft around mid-length, both elbows bent to keep the axe in, under the body. (For if it flies out at arm's length, you won't be able to press on it with your chest, which greatly aids in grinding the pick into the snow, and bringing you to a stop.) If you want your self arrest to work when you need it, better practice self arrests repeatedly on a safe slope with a good run-out. But treat the self arrest as a last resort: for an ice axe, well-planted at each step, will keep you from falling at all, should your feet slip out from under you. In roped glacier travel, without skis, you must fall into a self-arrest position to hold another climber who has fallen into a crevasse.

As in skiing, the key to snow-and-ice climbing, and rock climbing as well, is balance. You must keep your center of gravity directly over your feet. Leaning into the slope, from nervousness, will only make matters worse. In fact, when traversing moderately steep slopes, the ice axe is used as a sort of cross brace—propping you out from the slope and keeping you vertically above your feet.

On rock, the climber commonly progresses with his own hands and feet, not with external climbing tools like axe and crampons. His equipment (rope and hardware) is for safety and not for upward progress. Of course, there is also 'artificial climbing' which permits the ascent of nearly blank, holdless walls. But this is an advanced and specialized form of climbing, beyond the scope of our discussion. In fact, we'll limit ourselves now to naming the main rock climbing techniques, and not try to penetrate their secrets in this short space.

Friction climbing utilizes the adherence of the rubber soles of the climber's boots on holdless slabs of rock. *Face climbing* is most people's image of climbing—using ledge-like hand and foot holds (mostly sharp edges) to climb upward. *Jamming* means wedging part of your body—toe, foot or knee, fingers, fist, or arm—into a crack or fissure in the rock and using it for a hold. The jammed fist, or boot, or whatever, is held in the crack by cross-pressure against both walls of the crack. Climbers speak of *hand jams, foot jams*, and so forth. Two other techniques involve cross-pressure. *Chimneying*, or wedging the entire body into large

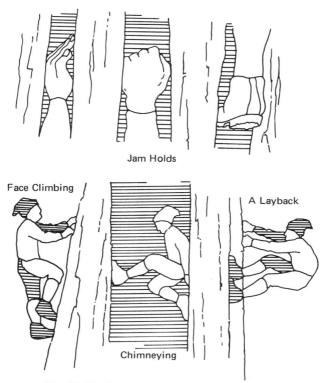

Jam Holds

Face Climbing

Chimneying

A Layback

Fig. 37. Typical Rockclimbing Techniques

cracks or chimneys. And *laybacking*—in which the hands and arms pull directly outward on a crack or edge, thus forcing the feet perpendicularly against the rock so that they can grip. All these techniques can be, and are, used in combination. But the most clever combinations usually involve some sort of cross-pressure—that is, one part of the body pushing or pulling against the opposite push or pull of another part.

How do you become a rock climber, or a snow-and-ice climber for that matter? Emphatically not by reading books, but by climbing. Yet because of the potential risks, you should start your climbing career under the guidance of experienced climbers, who will help you avoid many pitfalls and speed your progress. Numerous climbing and outdoor clubs have regularly scheduled practice climbs and training sessions. Take advantage of them. Or find someone to pass on the minimum safety skills, so you won't do yourself in while learning to climb. What are these minimum safety skills? Let's see.

USING THE ROPE: The nylon (or perlon) climbing rope is the climber's basic weapon for re-balancing the odds in his favor on steep dangerous terrain. Ropes for serious technical climbing are usually 11 mm. in diameter; for most mountaineering 9 mm. will do. These ropes vary in length from 120 to 150 feet. European perlon ropes of Kernmantel (sheath and core) construction are preferable for their ease of handling and resistance to wear. But American-made three-strand, laid nylon ropes (7/16" or 3/8") are acceptable, and cheaper.

The rope is used for *belaying*, or safeguarding, the climbing party. Traveling across a glacier, all members of a roped party move together; and they must react instantly when someone falls in. But falling 'in' is a lot less serious than falling 'off'; so on an actual climb, members of the party move one at a time. One climber, *the belayer*, anchors himself to a solid position. He may use the climbing rope, or auxillary slings (loops of strong nylon webbing or thin rope), tying himself to a horn of rock, a tree on the cliff, a chockstone (real or man-made) wedged into a crack, or a piton (metal spike) driven into a crack. On snow or ice, he may tie-in to his ice axe, or to ice pitons or tubular 'ice screws' driven or screwed into the slope. One belay on snow, the so-called boot-axe belay, is used without the belayer anchoring himself. The belayer tries to assume a position in which he is braced against the possible direction of pull (in case of a fall by the climber on the other end of the rope). The most solid position is sitting, feet braced in a wide triangular base, but this is often impossible to assume.

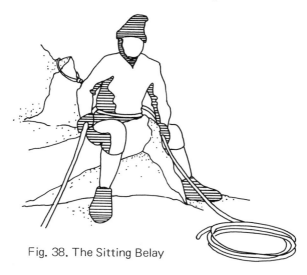

Fig. 38. The Sitting Belay

The more unstable the belayer's position, the tighter and more secure must be his anchor. (For a typical example, see fig. 38.)

Then, in order to belay the moving climber—either ascending above him ('leading') or else coming up beneath him ('following')—the belayer must pass the rope around his hips, and take it in or pay it out as the other climber moves. Thus his body acts somewhat like a hitching post, or friction device. He will hold any eventual fall with the hand that grasps the rope *after it has passed around his body*. But both hands are used for feeding out, or taking in the rope.

How does the belayer stop a fall? Just as you would think—by hanging onto the rope as tightly as possible. In past years, much has been made of a theory of so-called 'dynamic belaying'—the belayer consciously letting slack slide through his hands, in order slowly to absorb the energy of a falling climber. It's a fine theory, but it doesn't really work, nor is it necessary. Modern ropes have a dynamic stretching quality built into them. (They are relatively stiff under a low load, relatively elastic under a high load such as a fall.) The experience of numerous falls in Yosemite Valley, the Mecca of American rock climbing, has conclusively demonstrated that the belayer's *instinctive reaction*—to grip the rope as tightly as possible—is correct. Once the climber's fall has been stopped, he either must be lowered to a comfortable resting spot—or else brought back to the belayer's position, by means similar to those of crevasse rescue (prusik knots, etc.). If the fallen climber is unconscious or hurt, the belayer has a major task on his hands.

Obviously, it's the role of judgment to avoid such eventualities, and to limit the possible fall a climber may take.

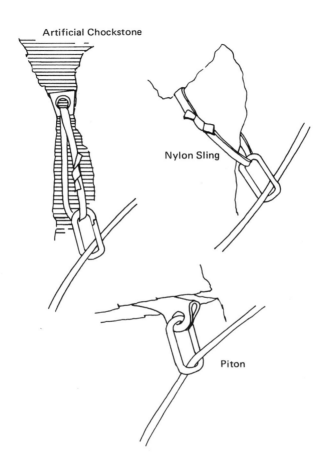

Fig. 39. Runners for Protecting the Leader

The second man, with a rope from above, is generally as safe as can be. It is the leader who is exposed. So, to limit the possible fall he might take, the leader passes his rope through intermediate belay points, or *runners*, that he establishes as he leads the *pitch* (the rope length). Such runners could be a sling around a horn of rock or tree, an artificial chockstone or 'nut' he has wedged into a crack, or a piton he has driven. The rope is 'clipped-in' to such runners with an aluminum snap link or *carabiner*. We won't describe the placement of such artificial runners on a pitch, or of anchors at a belay spot. This is an art in itself, covered in specialized texts, and one that must be mastered through much practice. Anyone can drive a piton, or place a nut. The trick is to know if it will hold.

Aluminum nuts, wedges, chocks, crackers, and so forth, are referred to as artificial chockstones, because they are fitted into cracks, where they wedge just like natural chockstones. These have only recently become popular in American climbing circles. But they are invaluable, for they are lighter than the traditional pitons, easier to place and remove, and leave no scars on the rock. We heartily recommend artificial chocks to the ski-touring mountaineer. (See fig. 39 for an illustration of the way some of these runners can be placed and used.)

While this is not by any means the whole story of belaying and technical climbing, it more-or-less covers the rough essentials. When the leader reaches the top of the pitch—that is, when he is running out of rope—he must find a stance or belay spot, anchor himself in, and belay the second man up to his stance. Then the process repeats. Two equally skilled climbers on the same rope often alternate, or 'swing' leads—the second man continuing as leader of the

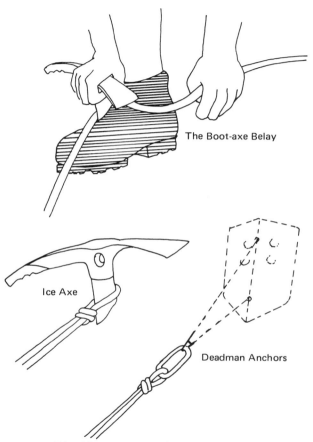

The Boot-axe Belay

Ice Axe

Deadman Anchors

Fig. 40. Belay Techniques for Snow

next pitch. Experienced climbers also reduce their shouted signals to an absolute minimum. 'On-belay' and 'off-belay' and 'climbing' should suffice. For serious climbing, a rope-team of two is standard. Three is possible but slower and more cumbersome, except for travel on crevassed glaciers, where, we've seen, the third man represents extra security.

In general, belays on snow and ice are less secure than on rock. On ice, one must belay from ice pitons, or ice screws which are stronger and easier to use in most cases. On snow, one has a choice. Either driving the ice axe in all the way, anchoring oneself to it, and belaying as usual with the rope running around the hips. Or using the ingenious boot-axe belay, in which the belayer's boot actually reinforces the strength of the axe. This boot-axe belay is probably preferable in most cases, and is shown in figure 40.

A recent innovation for snow climbing is the 'dead-man.' This is a sort of aluminum fluke (like a shovel blade) attached to a wire or sling and which can be buried in the snow to provide a fine anchor. Most snow belays are adequate for protecting the second man, coming up from below, but questionable for protecting a leader, high above.

The rope is also used for *rappelling*, or descending, over ground too steep to climb down. A solid rappel point is chosen to anchor the rope; and a nylon sling loop is passed through or around this point. The rope is passed through the sling, so that it hangs double down the pitch to be rappelled. When the climbers reach the bottom, they retrieve the rope by pulling one end. The sling at the top facilitates this pulling-down, which would often be impossible if the rope were passed directly around a tree or spike of rock.

A simple method of rappelling is shown in figure 41.

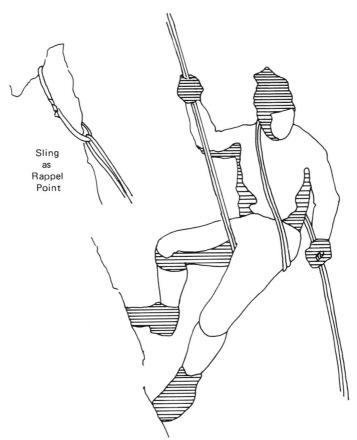

Sling
as
Rappel
Point

Fig. 41. The Classical Body Rappel

Although there are numerous variations, some much more comfortable, this classic rappel must be learned first. As in belaying, the hand holding the rope, after it has been wrapped around the body, is the one that does most of the work. It is the *braking hand*. The other one, held in front, has the important task of keeping the climber upright and in balance while he is rappelling.

In essence, you just walk backwards down the cliff, controlling your descent with your braking hand. The friction around your body makes this quite simple. *Never descend in large bounding leaps, but walk quietly and gently down the cliff*. This warning is addressed to beginners who usually think that rappelling is fun. If statistics are correct, rappelling is one of the most dangerous things you can do. More great alpinists have died in rappel accidents, than from any other single cause. While rappelling, your life is literally hanging from a thread. And experienced climbers often have the uncomfortable feeling that they are no longer in control of their own fate.

So be very careful in setting up any rappel. Always replace old rappel slings, left by other parties on a standard descent route, with new slings. The sling should not pass over sharp edges that might abrade it, and should be long enough so that it's easy to pull down the rope. Many experienced climbers rappel with a prusik knot on the rappel rope. They slide this prusik knot down with the front hand; and, attached to their waist by a sling, it will support them if, for example, they are knocked out by a rock falling from above. At any rate, take it easy and treat any rappel with great respect. We generally prefer to climb down, instead of rappelling, wherever possible.

Finally, let's just repeat what we said at the beginning of

this section. Climbing is an entirely different art, and you would do well to treat every phase of it with respect. For the climber generally plays for higher stakes than the skier. What you've just read is only an introduction to the subject—far from a proper text. But the authors (both of us as devoted to mountaineering as to wilderness skiing) hope this short summary of mountaineering techniques has been intriguing enough to whet your appetite for more. Of course, the real stimulus for becoming a mountaineer, as well as a ski tourer, is the sight of remote but ineffably attractive summits. Places where you'd like to go, but can't go yet.

This experience, this disturbing lure of the impossible, is common to all of us. No matter how skilled you become, skier or climber; no matter how 'fit' you are, how many miles you've already skied this winter—there's always a 'beyond.' A slope steeper than you've ever skied before. A peak that's higher or better defended than any you've ever visited. A ski tour longer and more challenging than any you've ever done. Of course, we don't have to spend all our time looking for such challenges. Nobody does. We don't even have to accept them, and wrestle with them. But as the adventures and the risks are slowly, one by one, eliminated from the social environment in which we live, it's somehow reassuring to know that there are natural challenges still out there waiting, only a snowfield or a rope length away.

11. Endless Winter

One of the best ways of preserving intact your finest moments on skis, surely, is to photograph them. The camera, as a tool for snatching away souvenirs, falls within the limits of the strictest wilderness ethic. For what it captures, in an arrangement of silver halides on an acetate base, is only a memory. Even our ski tracks are more obtrusive. They must be smoothed over and erased by wind and sun, melting and freezing, or by a forgiving blanket of new snow.

Let's end by sharing some photos of wilderness skiing that we've collected from friends across the country. They don't have anything to do with ski technique or snow camping. They are only simple souvenirs of an endless winter.

A

B

D

E

F

1

Photo credits

(A) Touring skiiers on the South Bowl of Mt. Bridger, Utah. By Pete Lev.

(B) Toward High Camp in the Sawtooth Sierra of California. By Lito Tejada-Flores.

(C) Skiing steep slopes near Lake Tahoe in California. By Lito Tejada-Flores.

(D) Ski camp near head of the Newton Glacier, Mt. St. Elias, British Columbia. By Alice Culbert.

(E) Ski touring in the Alps. By Toni Hiebeler.

(F) Spring avalanche in the Wasatch Mountains, Utah. By Alexis Kelner.

(G) More touring in the Alps. By Toni Hiebeler.

(H) On the broken Newton Glacier, Mt. Jeanette in background. By Alice Culbert.

(I) Harsh conditions on the lower Dinwoody Glacier, Wind River Range, Wyoming. By Alexis Kelner.

(J) Ski mountaineers below Gannet Peak (13,785 ft.), Wyoming's highest. By Alexis Kelner.

(K) Approaching Mt. Waddington, British Columbia. By Dick Culbert.

Appendices

A. Lists

1. An equipment checklist for ski touring

The following is not a list of things you *must* take. It is an all-inclusive list (too large really) of things you *might* want to take ski touring. You can use it as an *aide memoire*, for checking off the items you will need on a particular tour, under particular conditions. You may, of course, come up with things we've forgotten.

GEAR TO BE WORN:

    Long underwear, woolen or cotton
    String-net undershirt and longjohns
    Cotton shirt or turtle neck
    Wool shirt
    Ski sweater
    Down sweater or down jacket (with hood)
    Nylon wind shirt
    Outer wind parka (full length)
    Ski pants or knickers (with belt)
    Wind pants or coated-nylon 'powder pants'

Socks, heavy wool, light cotton, knee length, regular, plus an extra set (choose to suit your particular ski boot/pants combination)

Wool ski cap or balaklava helmet

Sun hat

Bandana or scarf

Dark glasses or goggles

Gaiters (preferably knee-high)

Gloves, a wide range of possibilities, including: leather ski gloves, silk liner gloves, Dachstein-type mitts of unwashed wool, waterproof nylon over-mitts, and down-filled mitts. (Choose according to the harshness of conditions you expect to encounter)

Watch

SKI GEAR:

Ski boots (possibly with innersoles of nylon mesh or sheepskin)

Skis and bindings (Check the *condition* of the bindings, for loose screws, missing straps, and so forth.)

Ski poles

Climbing Skins or waxes (usually a small wax kit carried in the pack)

GEAR NORMALLY CARRIED:

Day pack or light rucksack

Small emergency repair kit, or tool, for the skis

First aid kit

Sunburn protection for face and lips (and possibly spare goggles)

Water flask

Lunch food

Map and compass

Avalanche cord

Toilet kit as desired (including toilet paper)

A light waterproof plastic sheet, mini-tarp or space blanket, or even a nylon bivouac sack.

Camera and film (with yellow and red filters for snow scenes if using black-and-white film)

ADDITIONAL GEAR FOR SNOW CAMPING:

For each person:

Larger rucksack or packframe

Down sleeping bag

Foam sleeping pad

Large plastic cup/bowl for drinking and eating

Aluminum spoon

Down booties and nylon overboots, for wearing around camp

Small headlamp, or flashlight, and batteries

Matches (lots) and waterproof matches (just in case)

Community gear for the whole party:

Tent

Snow shovels

Stove, with funnel for filling

Fuel tins, *full* of gas

Two nesting aluminum pots, or 'scout kettles'

Several large cooking spoons

Pot-cleaning stuff (Brillo, plastic pads, paper towels, whatever.)

Food and food containers

Half-gallon plastic water flask

Repair kit and first aid kit: each expanded to meet the
   needs of a longer trip; only one for the whole party
A small sewing kit (included in the above repair kit)
Folding wire saw, for cutting dead wood to burn.
Spare ski tip

There is no end to what you can add to this list, but
remember you have to carry it—so take it easy. Possible
additional items might be: spare parts for stove and tent,
extra boot-laces, extra batteries, boot wax or sno-seal, ther-
mometer and altimeter, playing cards and folding chess set,
an inflatable splint, candles and fire-starting material, bamboo wands for marking glacier routes, paperback novels
which can be torn apart and shared (page by page) with the
whole group, and on and on.

EQUIPMENT FOR MOUNTAINEERING:

Climbing boots—that is, make sure your ski-touring
   boots have rubber profile soles suitable for climbing.
Ice axe and/or ice hammer
Crampons with straps attached
A small selection of climbing nuts (artificial chock-
   stones) on slings, and pitons
Aluminum carabiners (about twice as many as the num-
   ber of pitons and nuts you're carrying)
Half-dozen climbing slings or runners (loops of 1" nylon
   webbing) and perlon prusik loops
Nylon-webbing 'swami belts' for each climber
50 feet of ½" nylon webbing, for making rappel slings
Several 'dead men' or aluminum snow anchors
Perlon climbing rope

2. A general food list

STARCHES: Plan on 0.9 pounds per man-day of the following: Cereals: instant, quick-cooking or pre-cooked, such as Swiss muesli or 'Crunchy Granola'. Spaghetti, noodles or macaroni. Instant rice or instant potatoes, and bulgur wheat or pilaf. Breads: pumpernickel, other dark breads, biscuits, cookies, Logan bread, flour or corn tortillas. Powdered soups (Swiss brands like Maggi and Knorr, and Liptons), and dehydrated or freeze-dried vegetables (though not all are starchy).

SUGAR: Plan on 0.4 pounds per man per day in the form of: Granulated sugar, either white or dark. Candy: hard candies, fruit drops, chocolate and fudge, peanut brittle and other assorted goodies. Instant puddings, honey, dried fruits, etc.

PROTEIN: Count on 0.6 pounds per man per day from the following: Salami, tinned meats, tinned bacon, Canadian bacon, beef jerky. Freeze-dried meats: hamburgers, sausages or steaks. Bacon bars and meat bars. All sorts of cheeses. Powdered milk, and egg mixes.

FATS AND FATTY FOODS: You need only ¼ pound per man-day in the form of: Butter, peanut butter, meat bars, nuts, olive oil, etc.

BEVERAGES: Figure on 0.1 pound per man per day of the following: Instant coffee, tea, chocolate drink mixes. As well as fruit-drink powders and jello (as a hot drink before it 'jells').

SEASONINGS: No requirements here. Use your imagination and the following: Salt and pepper. Chili powder. Curry powder. Tomato paste and powder. And an unlimited number of spices.

3. A wilderness medical kit

It is impossible to define exactly the optimum first-aid kit for ski touring or mountaineering. For one thing, there's no point in taking more than you know how to use—equipment or medicaments. On our own trips, the first-aid material carried has ranged from nothing more than a roll of two-inch adhesive tape to a complete medical kit with which we could suture large lacerations, and which also contained a large number of drugs prescribed especially for mountain emergencies. The average, and quite adequate, first-aid kit falls somewhere between these two extremes.

As an example of how small and compact a *complete medical kit* can be, we are including here the contents of a small (2"x6"x8") aluminum box carried by our good friend, Doctor Gilbert Roberts, on all his wilderness jaunts. Gil was expedition doctor to the successful American Everest Expedition and has a wide background in mountain medicine. With the following items he believes he can deal with almost any medical emergency likely to crop up in the back country. Of course, the average layman wouldn't know what to do with many of the drugs in Gil's medical kit. But on long remote trips without a doctor, an intelligent layman, with a little coaching beforehand from an interested physician, can perform numerous specialized medical functions, both emergency diagnosis and treatment. Naturally, the names of some medicaments we'll cite are likely to change with time, as new brands and new drugs become available.

A SAMPLE MEDICAL KIT:

Basic Equipment:
1 roller gauze bandage, 4"
10 band-aids
1 package of Steri-strips (for butterfly-type sutures)
2 gauze compresses, 4"x4"
1 small scissors
1 small needle holder
3 silk sutures with needles, 20, 40, and 60
1 #15 scalpel blade
1 syringe with needle
1 extra 25-gauge needle
2 alcohol sponges
1 tracheotomy canula (tracheatome)
1 18-gauge Foley catheter

Medicaments and Drugs:
1 small tube of Mycolog cream, for itching, rashes, etc.
1 tube of Neo-decadron eye ointment for allergic eye problems
Tetracaine eyedrops
Gantrasin eye ointment for eye infections or injuries
12 Amapicillin pills (250 mg.), a broad-spectrum antibiotic
10 ½-grain Morphine tablets for injection (can be dissolved in a small amount of Xylocaine)
1 vial (5cc) of injectable Decadron (cortisone)

1 ampoule of injectable Compazine, for nausea and stomach cramps

1 vial (20cc) of injectable Xylocaine, a local anesthetic

1 ampoule of injectable adrenalin

1 ampoule of injectable Lanoxin (digitalis)

2 ampoules of injectable Lasix (a diuretic)

1 small plastic vial containing the following pills:

10 Aspirin with codeine, ½ grain, for pain, cough and diarrhea

5 Seconal, 1½ grains, for sleep in difficult circumstances

5 Salt tablets

5 Dexedrine tablets (not recommended for getting weak members of the party up to something, but occasionally useful in getting exhausted or 'psyched-out' ones back down!)

5 Chlor'trimeton tablets, 4 mg., for hay fever and allergies

(Wrapped around the outside of the 2"x6"x8" aluminum box in which all this fits, Gil carries a ¼" wire mesh splint (more useful on climbing trips than ski tours where improvised-splint material abounds), and a 4" elastic ace bandage.)

The above kit is a lot more compact than the doctor's traditional black bag and does essentially the same job. Of course, many drugs (that a doctor would prefer to inject) can also be given in tablet, capsule or pill form. The only useful item that doesn't fit inside Gil's tiny medical kit is the ubiquitous roll of two-inch wide adhesive tape (especially useful for torn pants).

Remember, this is *not* a list of what you should take — much less a suggestion that the untrained wilderness skier could use even half of these items — but merely an exemplar of a very complete wilderness medical kit that weighs *one pound*!

B. Bibliography

1. Ski technique & touring guides

Brady, Michael. *Nordic Touring and Cross-Country Skiing.* Dreyers Forlag, Oslo, 1971, 92 pages.

Brady, Michael and Lorns Skjemstad. *Waxing for Ski Touring and Cross-Country Racing.* A small pamphlet distributed by Eiger Sports, San Fernando, California, n.d.

Brunner, Hans and Alois Kalin. *Ski de Fond.* Editions Payot, Paris, 1971, 77 pages. A beautifully illustrated book on Nordic ski technique, although the French text will limit its appeal, except perhaps in French Canada.

Burhenne, H.J. *Sierra Spring Ski-Touring.* Mountain Press, San Francisco, 1971, 96 pages. One-day tours to 28 peaks.

Caldwell, John. *The New Cross-Country Ski Book.* Stephen Greene Press, Brattleboro, Vermont, 1971, 128 pages.

This is the finest book devoted exclusively to Nordic ski technique that we have seen. The author is coach of the U.S. Cross-country team.

Joubert, Georges. *Teach Yourself to Ski.* Aspen Ski Masters, Aspen, Colorado, 203 pages. Of all the books on Alpine ski technique, and there are many, this is the only one worth reading. Although not written with the touring skier in mind, it is a valuable, comprehensive and very readable book. And it will probably remain the masterpiece in this field until Joubert writes a new book.

Larson, Robert D. *Ski Touring Handbook.* United States Ski Association, Central Division, Chicago, Ill., 1972, 45 pages. A very handy pamphlet on touring areas, routes and general touring information for the midwest region.

Lederer, William J. and Joe Pete Wilson. *Complete Cross-Country Skiing and Ski Touring.* W.W. Norton and Company, New York, 1970, 184 pages. This book is less than complete. It only covers Nordic technique, not touring. But is very thorough and detailed in its explanation of basic maneuvers.

Mattesich, Rudolph (Editor). *Ski Touring Guide.* Ski Touring Council, Inc., Troy, Vermont, published yearly, about 55 pages. Describes ski tours in the east.

Mueller, Ted. *Northwest Ski Trails.* The Mountaineers, Seattle, 1968, 222 pages. This book describes 60 tours and ski areas, beautifully.

Pause, Walter. *Salute the Skier: the Hundred Best Ski Runs in the Alps.* Bob Laurie Books, New York, 1963, 211 pages. Invaluable for planning European tours.

Traynard, Phillipe and Charles. *Cimes et Neige, 102 Som-*

mets a Ski. B. Arthaud, Paris, 1971, 220 pages. A guide to 102 high-mountain ski tours in the French Alps, ranging from extremely easy to such desperate ventures as skiing the Aiguille d'Argentière by the *glacier de Milieu.*

2. Living in the wilderness environment

Brower, David R. (Editor). *Going Light—with Backpack or Burro.* Sierra Club, San Francisco, 1968.

Bunnelle, Hasse. *Food for Knapsackers and Other Trail Travelers.* Sierra Club, San Francisco, 1971.

Cunningham and Hanson. *Lightweight Camping Equipment and How to Make it.* Ward, Colorado, 1964. Appeared in paperback in 1968.

Kjellstrom, Bjorn. *Be Expert with Map and Compass.* American Orienteering Service, LaPorte, Indiana, 1967.

Manning, Harvey (Editor). *Mountaineering, the Freedom of the Hills.* The Mountaineers, Seattle, 1970, 430 pages. The most complete American book on mountains and mountain-craft yet. Rather long, and long-winded, but invaluable. Also includes climbing techniques.

U.S. Department of Agriculture. *Composition of Foods.* Agriculture Handbook #8, Washington D.C., revised edition 1963.

3. Snow and avalanches

Fraser, Colin. *The Avalanche Enigma.* Rand McNally, New York, 1966, 301 pages. Fascinating reading.

Gallagher, Dale G. *Snowy Torrents—Avalanche Accidents in*

the U.S., 1910-1966. U.S.D.A., Forest Service, Alta Avalanche Study Center, 1967.

LaChapelle, E.R. *The ABC of Avalanche Safety.* Highland Publishing Company, Colorado, 1961. A small paperback pamphlet.

Seligman, Gerald. *Snow Structures and Ski Fields.* London, 1936.

U.S. Department of Agriculture. *Snow Avalanches—A Handbook of Forecasting and Control Measures.* Agriculture Handbook #194, Washington, D.C., 1961.

4. Self help and first aid

Darvill, F.T., M.D. *Mountaineering Medicine.* Skagit Mountain Rescue Unit, Mt. Vernon, Washington, 1969.

Field, Ernest K. (Editor). *Mountain Search and Rescue Operations.* Grand Tetons National Park, 1965.

Lathrop, Theodore G., M.D. *Hypothermia: Killer of the Unprepared.* The Mazamas, Portland, Oregon, 1970, 23 pages.

Mariner, Wastl. *Mountain Rescue Techniques.* The Mountaineers, Seattle (originally published by the Austrian Alpine Club, Innsbruck), 1963.

Washburn, Bradford. *Frostbite.* American Alpine Club, New York, 1962. A small pamphlet, reprinted from the American Alpine Journal.

Wilkerson, James A. (Editor). *Medicine for Mountaineering.* The Mountaineers, Seattle, 1967, 350 pages. *The* book on the subject.

5. Mountaineering techniques

Blackshaw, Alan. *Mountaineering: from Hill Walking to Alpine Climbing.* Penguin Books, Harmondsworth, England, 1965.

Mandolf, Henry (Editor). *Basic Mountaineering.* San Diego Chapter of the Sierra Club, San Diego, California, 1965, 118 pages. A paperback pamphlet, unpretentious and informative.

Rebuffat, Gaston. *On Ice and Snow and Rock.* Oxford University Press, New York, 1971, 190 pages. Superbly illustrated.

Robbins, Royal. *Basic Rockcraft.* La Siesta Press, Glendale, California, 1970. A slim paperback, but the most authoritative to date. The author is working on a sequel, Advanced Rockcraft, which should be equally valuable.

Smith, Phil. *Knots for Mountaineering.* Twenty-nine Palms, California, revised edition 1967.

Wheelock, Walter. *Ropes, Knots and Slings.* La Siesta Press, Glendale, California, 1967.

6. Maps

Topographic maps may be ordered directly from the Denver District Office, United States Geological Survey, Denver Federal Center, Denver, Colo. 80225.

Field Notes

Field Notes

Field Notes

Field Notes

Field Notes

Field Notes

Field Notes

Field Notes

Field Notes